AF541001

Communication and Journalism

NIPA® GENX ELECTRONIC RESOURCES & SOLUTIONS P. LTD.
New Delhi-110 034

About the Authors

Dr Rizwana Malik, doctorate in Agricultural Extension from the University of Agricultural Sciences, Bangalore, Karnataka, has demonstrated good achievements in her academic and professional career. Qualifying the National Eligibility Test (NET) in 2004, she has contributed to agricultural research, particularly at the grassroots level, focusing on disseminating technology to benefit fishers in general and farmer community in particular. Dr Malik's multifaceted involvement encompasses not only organizing training sessions and publishing approximately 40 research papers with an emphasis on practical applications but also leading various research projects. Her commitment to community development and the implementation of agricultural practices is evident in her work, which aims to enhance the lives and skills of individuals within the fisheries and other allied sectors.

Dr Mudasir M Kirmani working as Assistant Professor in the Division of Social Sciences, FoFy, SKUAST-K, holds doctorate in computer sciences. He has been associated with various projects which have been implemented to benefit the society in general and farmer community in particular. He has published more than 60 research articles, 02 books, and a good number of book chapters in reputed international publications.

Ms Reeba is a research scholar in Fisheries Extension at Division of Social Sciences, Faculty of Fisheries, SKUAST-K. She has completed her Bachelors in Fisheries Sciences and is pursuing her Masters in Fisheries Sciences where she has been associated with the different research projects of the division which has helped her to gain good acumen of research and reaching to fishers. She is an extensive researcher and has been actively involved in interacting with the fishers to help them in improving their knowledge and expertise.

Mr Moin Farooq is a research scholar in Fisheries Extension at Division of Social Sciences, Faculty of Fisheries, SKUAST-K. He has completed his Bachelors in Fisheries Sciences and is pursuing his Masters in Fisheries Sciences He is an extensive researcher and has been actively involved in interacting with the fishers to help them in improving their knowledge and expertise. He has been implementing the philosophy of "Empowering people around him to empower himself" while interacting with the farming community.

Communication and Journalism

Rizwana Malik
Associate Professor
Division of Social Sciences
Faculty of Fisheries
Sher-e-Kashmir University of Agricultural Sciences and Technology-Kashmir
Jammu and Kashmir, India

Mudasir M Kirmani
Assistant Professor
Division of Social Sciences
Faculty of Fisheries
Sher-e-Kashmir University of Agricultural Sciences and Technology-Kashmir
Jammu and Kashmir, India

Reeba Rouf
Research Scholar
Division of Social Sciences
Faculty of Fisheries
Sher-e-Kashmir University of Agricultural Sciences and Technology-Kashmir
Jammu and Kashmir, India

Moin Farooq
Research Scholar
Division of Social Sciences
Faculty of Fisheries
Sher-e-Kashmir University of Agricultural Sciences and Technology-Kashmir
Jammu and Kashmir, India

NIPA® GENX ELECTRONIC RESOURCES & SOLUTIONS P. LTD.
New Delhi-110 034

NIPA. GENX ELECTRONIC RESOURCES & SOLUTIONS P. LTD.

101,103, Vikas Surya Plaza, CU Block
L.S.C.Market, Pitam Pura, New Delhi-110 034
Ph. +91 11 27341616, 27341717, 27341718
E-mail: newindiapublishingagency@gmail.com
www: www.nipabooks.com

For customer assistance, please contact
Phone: + 91-11-27 34 17 17
Fax: + 91-11-27 34 16 16
E-Mail: feedbacks@nipabooks.com

Print ISBN: 978-93-58879-61-2

ebook ISBN: 978-93-58878-82-0

Sher-e-Kashmir
University of Agricultural Sciences & Technology of Kashmir
www.skuastkashmir.ac.in

Prof. Nazir A. Ganai
Vice-Chancellor

Foreword

Welcome to the amazing world of journalism and communication! You are going to experience the exciting world of idea expression. News Writing, storytelling and employing good communication to impact the world as you set off on your educational journey.

There has never been a more important role for media and communication in the fast-paced, globally connected world. With dedication, this book is meant to be your guide, offering you knowledge, insights, and useful skills that will help you advance in the journalism and communication industries.

Communication is an art, a science, and a skill that can be developed and perfected. It is not merely about conveying information. The concepts presented in this book will serve as your guide regardless of your career goals.

Within these pages, you will explore media literacy, ethical journalism, effective storytelling and the dynamic field of digital communication. We will investigate how narratives, pictures, and words can influence public opinion and create deep connections.

As students, you are on the front of creative thinking, equipped with the means to make sense of an information-rich environment. You can become the storytellers, activists, and communicators that our society needs if you have knowledge, curiosity, and a commitment to the truth. Communication and journalism provide a wide range of opportunities and challenges.

I hope that this book will support you all through your academic career by encouraging you to think critically, communicate clearly and make a significant contribution to the rapidly changing fields of journalism and communication.

(NazirAhmad Ganai)

Place: Shalimar, Srinagar

Dated: 21.12.2023

Preface

Greetings and welcome to a comprehensive exploration into the fields of journalism, media, and communication. This book takes the reader on a dynamic trip across the intersection of information, technology, and society progress.

We explore the foundational ideas of communication in the first few chapters setting the stage for a more sophisticated comprehension of its complex nature. From there, we continue our investigation into the dynamic field of media, paying close attention to how it both shapes and reflects societal shifts.

"Understanding the Structure and Construction of News" is an essential component that offers insights into the anatomy of news by removing the layers involved in its formation. Here, we walk through the fundamentals of news production, covering everything from moral dilemmas to the game-changing effects of technological advancements.

The focus of the ensuing chapters is the rich and diverse discipline of journalism. We examine all of its dimensions, from the conventional ideas that serve as its foundation to the opportunities and problems of the modern era brought about by the constantly evolving media landscape.

Finally, we look at the media's complex role in the larger social framework. This section examines the different ways that media affects and is influenced by the world in which it exists.

This book is written for students who are keen to understand the intricacies of journalism, media, and communication. We hope that this trip will encourage critical thinking about the significant impact that these fields have on the evolution of our societies, in addition to expanding your intellectual horizons.

Happy reading!

Authors

Preface

Contents

1

Communication

1.1 Meaning

The English word ‘communication’ is derived from the Latin communis, which means common sense. In other words, it is the transmission and interaction of facts, ideas, opinions, feelings, or attitudes. Communication is a two-way process that involves transferring info rmation or messages from one person or group to another. This process goes on and includes a minimum of one sender and receiver to pass on the messages. These messages can either be any ideas, imagination, emotions, or thoughts. Communication is a Latin word that means “to share”.

1.2 Definitions

1. Communication is a process by which two or more persons exchange ideas, facts, and impressions in a way that each gains a common understanding of the meaning, context, and use of the message. -J. Paul, Leagan
2. All the procedures by which one mind can affect another. -Shanna & Weaver
3. Communication is a purposeful process, which involves sources, messages, channels, and receivers. - Andersch et al.
4. Communication is a process of transmitting and receiving verbal and non-verbal messages. It is considered effective when it achieves the desired response or reaction from the receiver -Murphy, Hildebrandt, Thomas

1.3 Communication Meaning in the Context of Extension

In the context of extension services, communication refers to the systematic and strategic exchange of information, knowledge, and skills between extension professionals (extension workers or agents) and the target audience, which may include farmers, rural communities, or other stakeholders. This communication aims to facilitate the adoption of improved practices, technologies, and innovations to enhance agricultural productivity, rural development, and overall well-being.

1.4 Importance of Communication in Extension

- **Information Dissemination:** Delivering current information, research findings, and best practices to the target audience is primarily done through communication. It makes sure that farmers and others living in rural areas are informed about the most recent advancements in agriculture and related industries.

- **Education and Capacity Building:** Extension communication plays a crucial role in educating individuals and communities, equipping them with the knowledge and skills necessary to make informed decisions and improve their livelihoods.
- **Behaviour Change**: Extension communication is essential for educating people and communities, giving them the information and abilities needed to make wise decisions and enhance their quality of life.
- **Problem Solving:** Communication enables the identification and discussion of particular difficulties and problems faced by farmers. The target population and extension specialists can collaborate to find workable solutions.
- **Participatory Decision-**Making: Engaging in two-way communication ensures that the voices and opinions of farmers and community members are heard. It empowers them to actively participate in the decision-making process.
- **Feedback and Adaptation:** Extension communication should be a two-way street, enabling farmers to provide feedback on the effectiveness of the extension services and to voice their concerns or needs. This feedback loop allows for program adjustments and improvements.
- **Empowerment**: Individuals and groups are empowered by communication because it gives them knowledge and information, boosts their self-reliance, and gives them the self-assurance to manage their resources wisely.
- **Sustainability**: Good communication promotes the adoption of environmentally friendly and sustainable practices, which helps with rural development and the long- term conservation of resources.
- **Social and Cultural Relevance**: Communication methods should be culturally sensitive and consider local customs and traditions, ensuring that messages resonate with the target audience.
- **Technology Transfer:** In modern extension services, communication includes the use of various technologies, such as mobile apps, SMS messages, and radio broadcasts, to extend information to remote and underserved areas.

- **Community Development**: Extension communication can promote community togetherness and cooperation, resulting in group efforts for common objectives and development activities.
- **Policy Advocacy:** Extension services can use communication to advocate for policy changes or to inform policymakers about the needs and challenges of rural communities.
- **Monitoring and Evaluation**: Good communication is crucial for gathering information and getting feedback so that extension programme efficacy can be assessed and future interventions may be chosen based on the best available data.

The foundation of successful knowledge transfer and rural development in extension services is good communication. It supports sustainable practices, empowers communities to improve their quality of life, and aids in closing the knowledge gap between specialists and farmers. To make sure that their words are heard, accepted, and successfully adopted by the target audience, extension workers need to have great communication skills.

1.5 Perspectives in Communication

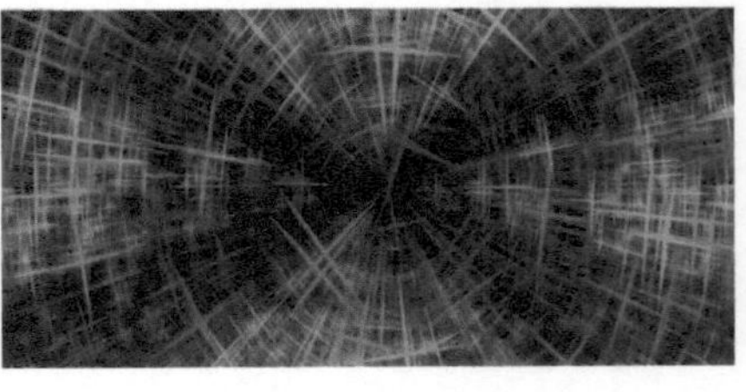

- **Information Dissemination Perspective:** According to this perspective, communication is a mechanism by which knowledge, technical data, and research findings are disseminated by specialists to farmers and rural communities. Communication is a key tool that extension specialists utilize to share the most recent information, industry best practices, and solutions to problems in agriculture and rural development.
- **Educational Perspective:** Communication in extension is seen as an educational tool. It involves teaching and capacity building, helping individuals and communities acquire the necessary knowledge and skills to make informed decisions, improve their livelihoods, and adopt new agricultural practices.
- **Behaviour Change Perspective:** It takes excellent communication to encourage behaviour change. Extension agents use communication to persuade farmers and other stakeholders to embrace new practices innovations, and approaches. It focuses on emphasizing the benefits of using specific actions or strategies.

- **Participatory Perspective:** In a participatory communication approach the emphasis is on engaging the target audience actively in the decision-making process. Communication becomes a two-way interaction that encourages dialogue, collaboration, and shared decision-making between extension professionals and farmers.
- **Empowerment Perspective:** People see communication as a means of empowerment, especially in rural and marginalized populations. It gives people knowledge, information, and a sense of empowerment so they may take charge of their resources, make wise decisions, and live better lives.
- **Cultural and Contextual Perspective:** Effective communication in extension recognizes the significance of culture and context. It considers local customs, traditions, and social norms when crafting messages and interventions. It ensures that communication is culturally sensitive and relevant to the target audience.
- **Technology Transfer Perspective:** With the progress of technology, agricultural innovations are being disseminated through a range of media, such as online platforms, radio, SMS, and mobile apps, as part of extension communication. This viewpoint highlights the use of technology to provide information and services to underserved and rural areas.
- **Community Development Perspective:** From this viewpoint, communication fosters community development by encouraging collaboration, problem-solving, and collective actions. It brings communities together to address shared challenges and achieve common goals.
- **Social Change Perspective:** In rural communities, communication is key to advocating for social and political change. Extension specialists utilize communication as a weapon to affect policy decisions, rally public support for social causes, and broaden people's understanding of pertinent issues.
- **Sustainability Perspective:** The foundation of this viewpoint is the management of natural resources and sustainable agriculture. The adoption of ecologically beneficial practices and conservation measures is encouraged via communication, which benefits rural people and ecosystems over the long run.

- **Policy Advocacy Perspective:** Policymakers can be informed about the demands and difficulties faced by rural communities through communication, or it can be used to advocate for policy changes. To solve systemic problems affecting agriculture and rural development, extension services may participate in policy discussions.
- **Monitoring and Evaluation Perspective:** Gaining information and receiving feedback to evaluate the success of extension programs requires effective communication. This viewpoint emphasizes the use of communication to assess the efficacy of interventions and make data-driven programme decisions in the future.

These various perspectives on communication in extension reflect the multifaceted role it plays in rural development, knowledge transfer, and agricultural sustainability. Extension services often incorporate a combination of these perspectives to address the complex and evolving needs of farmers and rural communities.

1.6 Characteristics of Communication

Characteristics of communications are given below:

- **Two or More Persons**: A minimum of two persons must be involved in communication since one person cannot exchange thoughts with themselves. This is communication's first important characteristic. Someone has to pay attention to what you have to say. Therefore, at least two persons must be present for the information to be given and received.
- **Exchange of Ideas**: The interchange of ideas is necessary for communication to even occur. Exchanges of thoughts, instructions, emotions, and other information between two or more people are necessary for communication to be completed.
- **Mutual Understanding**: Mutual understanding is the idea that the recipient of the knowledge ought to receive it in the same spirit that it is being offered. In communication, comprehending the material is more important than doing it.
- **Direct and Indirect Communication**: It is not essential for the sender and the recipient of information to have face-to-face communication. It is possible to communicate directly or indirectly. Face-to-face interactions are considered direct communication, whilst other channels are considered indirect.

- **Continuous Process**: Communication is an ongoing process, much like in a professional context where a manager routinely gives directions assigns projects to subordinates, and keeps track of the work's progress.
- **Use of Words as well as Symbols**: There are numerous more ways to communicate, including written, oral, and symbolic methods. Using your finger to indicate a cricket match, nodding your head, glaring at someone to show wrath or displeasure, or ringing a bell to close a business or school are examples of symbolic communication.

1.7 Communication Process

Communication is a complex process that involves several key elements working together to convey messages from a sender to a receiver. These elements are essential for understanding the dynamics of communication. Here are the primary elements of communication:

- **Sender**: The sender, who is sometimes referred to as the communicator or source, starts the communication by producing a message. Any entity that wishes to share information or ideas may be an individual, a group an organization, etc.
- **Message:** The message is the content or information that the sender wishes to communicate. It can be conveyed through various means, including verbal language, written text, images, sounds, or non-verbal cues.
- **Encoding:** Encoding requires converting the communication into a format or code that can be sent to the recipient. To effectively communicate a message, this may entail making word choices, producing images, or employing symbols.
- **Channel:** The medium or mechanism utilized to transfer the message from the sender to the receiver is known as the channel. Face-to-face interactions, written correspondence, electronic mail, social media phone calls, video conferencing, and more are examples of common channels.
- **Decoding:** Decoding is the process by which the receiver interprets and makes sense of the message. It involves understanding the encoded message and extracting meaning from it.

- **Receiver:** The person, entity, or group receiving the message is referred to as the receiver. They are responsible for deciphering and interpreting the communication. The receiver's comprehension of the message affects how well a message is received.
- **Feedback:** Feedback is the response or reaction provided by the receiver to the sender. It allows the sender to assess whether the message was understood and received as intended. Feedback can be verbal or non-verbal.
- **Noise:** Noise refers to any interference, distraction, or barriers that may disrupt or distort the communication process. Noise can be external (e.g., background noise, technical issues) or internal (e.g., biases, emotions, distractions).
- **Context:** The context provides the setting and circumstances in which the communication takes place. It includes the physical environment, cultural and social factors, and the relationship between **the sender and receiver.**
- **Feedback Loop:** Effective communication often involves a feedback loop, where the receiver provides feedback, and the sender adjusts the message or delivery based on that feedback. This loop ensures that the message is understood and received as intended.
- **Medium:** The medium refers to the specific form or technology used for communication, such as text messages, emails, face-to-face conversations, or visual presentations. The choice of medium can affect the effectiveness of communication.
- **Barriers:** Communication barriers are obstacles that can hinder the flow of information between the sender and receiver. Common barriers include language differences, cultural misunderstandings, technical issues, and emotional barriers.
- **Purpose:** Every communication has a purpose or goal, whether it's to inform, persuade, entertain, express emotions, or engage in dialogue. The purpose shapes the content and style of the message.
- **Non-Verbal Communication**: Non-verbal communication refers to the transmission of messages or information without using words. It involves conveying thoughts, feelings, or ideas through facial expressions, gestures, body language, posture, eye contact, and other forms of expression. Essentially, it's the way we communicate without

speaking or writing. Non-verbal cues can provide important insights into a person's emotions, attitudes, and intentions, and they play a significant role in human interaction.

Understanding and managing these elements of communication is vital for effective and meaningful interactions. Effective communicators consider these elements to ensure that their messages are clear, well-received, and free from misinterpretation. Additionally, awareness of potential barriers and context helps facilitate better communication.

1.8 Types of Communication

In the context of extension services, individual, group, and mass communication play essential roles in disseminating agricultural knowledge, promoting rural development, and engaging with different stakeholders. Here's how these forms of communication are applied in extension:

Individual Communication in Extension

Definition: Individual communication in extension refers to one-on-one exchanges between extension specialists (agents) and specific farmers or community members. It is customized and tailored to the recipient's particular requirements and situation.

Application

- Extension agents pay visits to farms or families to offer individual farmers tailored advice, guidance, and training.
- Providing farmers with targeted challenges with technical support and problem-solving expertise. creating personalized farm plans and carrying out individual requirements evaluations.
- Text messages, phone calls, or emails address particular issues or queries.

Group Communication in Extension

Definition: Interactions with small to medium-sized groups of farmers or community members constitute group communication in extension. The group's discussions and knowledge-sharing are facilitated by extension workers.

Application

- Organizing farmer field days, workshops, and training sessions to educate groups of farmers on specific topics.
- Facilitating group discussions, knowledge-sharing sessions, and farmer-to-farmer learning.
- Forming and leading agricultural producer groups or cooperatives to promote collective decision-making and resource sharing.
- Conducting group-based demonstrations of new agricultural practices.

Mass Communication in Extension

Definition: In extension, mass communication includes reaching a large and varied audience, frequently via mass media channels or technologies. Mass media is one tool that extension services utilize to communicate with the public, disseminate information, and increase awareness.

Application

- In extension, mass communication includes reaching a large and varied audience.
- frequently via mass media channels or technologies.
- Mass media is one tool that extension services utilize to communicate with the public, disseminate information, and increase awareness.
- Using websites and social media channels to communicate with a wider online community and spread information.
- Introducing public awareness campaigns or advertisements to highlight important extension messages.

Each form of Communication in Extension Serves Specific Purposes

- **Individual communication** allows for personalized support and tailored solutions to address the unique needs of individual farmers.
- **Group communication** fosters peer learning and collaboration within smaller community groups, promoting the exchange of local knowledge and best practices.
- **Mass communication** helps extension services reach a wider audience, disseminate general information, and raise awareness about important agricultural and rural development issues.

Effective extension programs often combine all three forms of communication to ensure comprehensive coverage and engagement with various stakeholders, addressing both individual and collective needs in the process of agricultural and rural development.

1.9 Directions of Communication

Upward, downward, and horizontal communication are distinct levels or directions of communication within an organization. They describe how information, messages, and feedback flow among individuals or groups at different organizational levels or within the same hierarchical level. Here's a more detailed explanation of each level:

Upward Communication

Definition: Upward communication refers to the flow of information, messages, or feedback from subordinates, lower- level employees, or front-line workers to higher-level management, supervisors, or decision-makers in the organization.

Characteristics

- It acts as a means for staff members to communicate with supervisors, discuss ideas, voice concerns, and provide feedback.
- Often utilized for revealing problems seeking advice, exchanging recommendations, and conveying daily difficulties.
- Improves employee participation, engagement, and involvement in decision-making procedures.

Examples

The supervisor or manager reviews the email and, recognizing the value of the suggestion, decides to escalate it further up the hierarchy. They forward the email and their endorsement to the department head or a relevant higher-level authority.

In this example, upward communication allows the employee to share valuable insights and suggestions for process improvement with the organization's leadership. It demonstrates how employees can contribute to the organization's growth and efficiency by providing feedback and ideas to their superiors, ultimately benefiting the company as a whole.

Downward Communication

Definition: Downward communication involves the transmission of information, directives, instructions, policies, decisions, and guidance from higher-level management, supervisors, or executives to lower-level employees, teams, or subordinates.

Characteristics

- Typically used for conveying organizational goals, objectives, expectations, strategies, and guidelines to the workforce.
- Facilitates the implementation of company policies and ensures alignment with the organization's vision and goals.
- Requires clear and effective communication to ensure that messages are understood and followed by all levels.

Examples

- Managers communicating company goals and objectives to their teams.
- Executives issuing directives, policies, or announcements to all employees.
- Supervisors providing instructions, task assignments, and project guidelines to their teams.

Horizontal Communication

Definition: Horizontal communication, also known as lateral communication, refers to the exchange of information, messages, or feedback between individuals or departments at the same hierarchical level or within the same organizational or functional level.

Characteristics

- It supports collaboration, coordination, and the sharing of information between colleagues or departments that work at the same organizational level.
- Facilitates problem-solving, idea-sharing, and the resolution of issues that may not require the involvement of higher management.
- Encourages cross-functional and cross-departmental teamwork and knowledge exchange.

Examples

- Colleagues from different departments collaborating on a joint project or initiative.
- Team members within the same department share updates, insights, and knowledge.
- Interactions between peers at the same organizational level to address common concerns and solve shared problems.

Clear and effective communication in all three directions—upward, downward, and horizontal—is crucial for the smooth operation and success of an organization. Each level of communication serves unique purposes and contributes to overall productivity, employee engagement, and the alignment of all members with the organization's goals and values.

1.10 Message

Definition: A message is the information or content that is sent throughout a communication process from a sender to a recipient. It can be expressed in a variety of ways, such as through spoken or written words, pictures, sounds gestures, or other symbols.

Characteristics

- Depending on the material being conveyed, messages might be straightforward or complex.
- Facts, thoughts, emotions, requests, directions, and other forms of communication can all be transmitted through messages.
- A message's effectiveness is determined by its relevance, clarity, and intended effect on the recipient.

Dimensions

- **Verbal Dimension:** This relates to the words used in the message. It includes the choice of vocabulary, grammar, and syntax. The way the message is structured verbally can impact its clarity and effectiveness.
- **Non-Verbal Dimension:** Non-verbal communication includes body language, facial expressions, gestures, tone of voice, and other non-

verbal cues. These elements convey emotions, emphasis, and additional meaning beyond the words themselves.

- **Visual Dimensions:** Information is communicated visually through the use of pictures, graphs, charts, symbols, and other visual components. It is frequently utilized in ads, data visualization, and presentations.
- **Contextual Dimension:** To fully comprehend a message, one must grasp the context in which it is conveyed. Setting, sender and receiver relationships, cultural norms, and communication timing are all context-related elements.
- **Emotional Dimension**: Messages can carry emotional content. Words and non-verbal cues can convey feelings, attitudes, and emotional states. Understanding and managing the emotional dimension is essential for effective communication.
- **Cultural Dimension:** Cultural factors play a significant role in determining the meaning of a message. Different cultures may interpret messages differently, leading to potential misunderstandings if not considered.

The way communication is formed, communicated, and perceived is influenced by its dimensions taken as a whole. A clear, accurate message that conveys the intended meaning and coincides with what the recipient understands are all components of effective communication, and they must be carefully considered. Furthermore, effective communication in a variety of contexts depends on an understanding of how cultural and contextual elements affect meaning.

1.11 Message Distortion

During the communication process, a message's substance, meaning, or intent may be altered without the sender's knowledge or consent. This is referred to as message distortion, also known as message misunderstanding or message distortion. This distortion can happen at several phases of communication and may be caused by biases, noise, misconception, or other issues. The following are some typical reasons for message distortion:

- **Misunderstanding**: Because of confusing or ambiguous wording, cultural differences, or the use of jargon or technical phrases that the recipient is unfamiliar with, the recipient may misinterpret the message.
- **Selective Perception:** Individuals tend to pay attention to specific aspects of a message that align with their preconceived beliefs or interests while

ignoring or downplaying other information. This selective perception can lead to a distortion of the message's original meaning.

- **Biases and Stereotypes:** The recipient's interpretation of a communication may be influenced by their own prejudices, assumptions or preconceptions. These biases could lead to misunderstandings or incorrect interpretations of the message.
- **Emotional States**: Emotional states, such as anger, stress, or anxiety, can affect how a message is perceived. When individuals are emotionally charged, they may misinterpret or distort messages due to their heightened emotional state.
- **Noise and Interference:** Environmental or internal noise, such as interruptions, background noise, technological difficulties, or competing messages, can interfere with communication and result in message misunderstanding or distortion.
- **Cultural Differences:** Differences in cultural norms, values, and communication styles can lead to misunderstandings and distortions of messages, especially in cross-cultural communication.
- **Incomplete Information**: Incomplete or missing context in a message can cause the recipient to fill in the gaps with assumptions, which can result in distortions.
- **Contextual Factors:** A message can be interpreted incorrectly or be misinterpreted depending on the communication environment, which includes the relationship between the sender and the recipient as well as the physical surroundings.

To minimize message distortion, effective communicators can employ strategies such as:

- It is important to use unambiguous language, encourage honest and open communication, and provide context and background knowledge as needed.
- Ensure comprehension by actively listening.
- Looking for explanations and comments.
- Being aware of potential biases and stereotypes.
- Adapting communication style to the needs and cultural background of the audience.

In some cases, it may be necessary to confirm that the message was correctly received and understood to prevent misunderstandings and distortions. Clear and effective communication is essential to minimize message distortion and ensure that the intended message aligns with the received message.

1.12 Barriers to Communication

Communication barriers are obstacles or challenges that make it difficult for individuals or groups to communicate ideas, information, or messages efficiently. These barriers can arise at many stages of the communication process and impair the efficacy, clarity, and comprehension of the message. Typical communication barriers include the following:

- **Language Barriers:** Communication can be hindered by disparities in language and vocabulary, especially in contexts that are multicultural or multilingual. Language barriers can also arise when industry- specific phrases or technical jargon are used, which may not be understood by the audience.
- **Cultural Barriers:** Cultural barriers can arise from variations in conventions, attitudes, and communication styles, which can cause miscommunication and misconceptions. Different cultures may interpret non- verbal signs, gestures, and rituals differently, which can lead to communication challenges.
- **Physical Barriers:** Physical impediments that impede communication include noise, distance, and technical difficulties.

  The message may be hard to hear or interpret due to background noise poor audio quality, or communication channel interruptions.
- **Psychological Barriers:** Receiving and interpreting a communication can be influenced by psychological elements such as emotional states, biases, prior assumptions, and personal views. Ineffective communication can be impeded by negative emotions such as stress, fear, or rage.
- **Semantic Barriers:** Misunderstandings or incorrect interpretations of words, phrases, or symbols are examples of semantic obstacles.

  Semantic obstacles can be caused by ambiguity, imprecise language, or words having numerous meanings.
- **Perceptual Barriers:** Perception and perspective variations might impact the comprehension of a communication. Perceptual obstacles may arise due to differences in an individual's attention, focus, and awareness levels.

- **Information Overload:** People who are overloaded with information may find it difficult to sort or prioritize communications.

  Information overload can result in selective attention and the neglect of important details.

- **Lack of Feedback:** The absence of feedback might result in assumptions and misunderstandings.

  Effective communication frequently depends on feedback to ensure that the message is interpreted as intended.

- **Organizational Barriers:** Organizational hierarchies, rules, and structures can obstruct communication.

  Transparency issues or bureaucratic procedures can impede candid and open communication.

- **Personal Barriers:** Personal factors such as a lack of communication skills, shyness, or a reluctance to speak up can hinder effective communication.

Some individuals may struggle with assertiveness or active listening.

Overcoming communication barriers requires awareness, active effort, and effective communication strategies. This may include using clear and simple language, providing context and explanations, active listening, cultural sensitivity, and fostering open and trusting relationships. Organizations can also implement policies and practices that promote effective communication and remove structural barriers.

1.13 Noise

In communications, "noise" is any disruptio interference, or distortion that reduces the effectiveness and clarity of communication. At various stages of communication, noise may express itself in a variety of ways. The list of common communication noises is as follows:

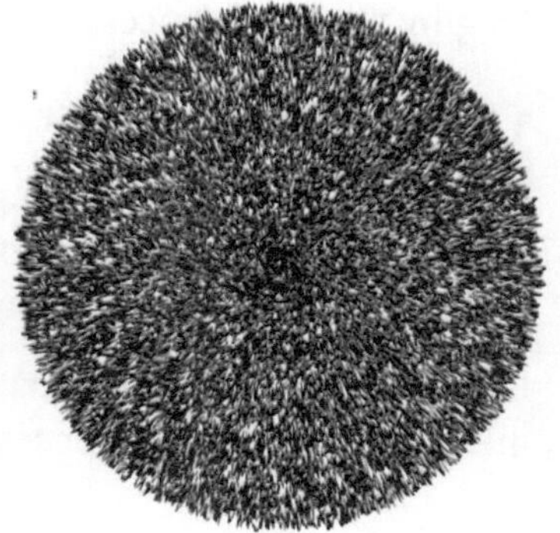

- **Physical Noise**

Definition: Physical noise is an outside component in the environment that interferes with communication. Any interference that makes challenging for the sender's message to reach the recipient without being distorted is included.

Examples: Background noise, loud music, machinery sounds, poor acoustics in a room, or technical issues like static in a phone call.

- **Semantic Noise**

Definition: Semantic noise arises from differences in the meaning of words or symbols used by the sender and receiver. It occurs when the choice of words, language, or terminology is not mutually understood.

Examples: Misunderstandings due to language barriers, jargon, or technical terms that are unfamiliar to the receiver.

- **Psychological Noise**

Definition: The emotional or psychological condition of the sender or receiver, which may have an impact on how they interpret or react to the communication, is the cause of psychological noise.

Examples: Stress, anger, fear, personal biases, preconceived notions, or emotional distractions that hinder the ability to focus on the message.

- **Cultural Noise**

Definition: Cultural noise arises from differences in cultural norms, values, and communication styles between the sender and receiver, leading to potential misunderstandings. **Examples:** Variations in non-verbal communication, customs, and social etiquette that may cause misinterpretation or offense.

- **Organizational Noise**

Definition: Organizational noise is related to the structural or administrative aspects of an organization that can hinder communication. It may include bureaucracy, hierarchical barriers, and complex administrative procedures.

Examples: Excessive layers of management, unclear reporting structures, or lengthy approval processes that slow down communication.

- **Channel-Related Noise**

Definition: Problems relating to the channel or medium that is utilized for communication are referred to as channel-related noise. Noise can be introduced by technical issues, low signal quality, or communication tool constraints.

For example, dropped calls on a cell phone, illegible text messages, and interrupted video conferences brought on by unreliable internet access

- **Physiological Noise**

Definition: Physical attributes or conditions of the transmitter or receiver that impact communication are connected to physiological noise. Health problems, hearing problems, or language difficulties could be among them.

For example, a person with hearing loss who finds it difficult to comprehend spoken messages or a sender whose speech is affected by a sore throat.

Understanding and mitigating noise is crucial for effective communication. To reduce noise, individuals can take steps such as using clear and simple language, seeking feedback to ensure understanding, adjusting communication to the receiver's needs, and managing emotional and psychological distractions. Organizations can also implement practices and technologies to minimize noise in their communication processes.

1.14 Key Communicators

In the context of extension services and agricultural or rural development, key communicators are individuals or entities who play a significant role in disseminating information, providing guidance, and influencing the adoption of new practices or technologies among farmers, rural communities, and stakeholders. Key communicators in extension services include:

- **Agricultural Extension Agents:** are professionals who work for the government or non- governmental organizations and are equipped to provide farmers with the latest agricultural methods, equipment, and information. They are vital communicators who work with farmers to advance their skills and knowledge.
- **Local Farmers and Farmer Groups:** are important sources of information for their communities, as they are seasoned farmers who have effectively incorporated modern agricultural technologies and practices. They are significant change agents because they impart their wisdom and experiences to other farmers.
- **Community Leaders:** Leaders in rural areas, such as village elders or cooperative executives, can play a crucial role in distributing information and organizing the local population for extension operations.
- **Non-Governmental Organizations (NGOs):** NGOs working in rural development often employ extension workers who serve as key communicators to deliver services, education, and resources to local communities.

- **Agricultural Researchers and Academics**: Scientists, researchers, and academics in the field of agriculture serve as key communicators by sharing research findings, innovative practices, and updated knowledge with farmers and stakeholders.
- **Agricultural Cooperatives**: Farmer cooperatives and associations play a vital role in organizing and educating members, promoting best practices, and serving as key communicators in agricultural communities.
- **Government Agencies**: Government agricultural departments and agencies disseminate information on policies, regulations, and support programs, making them important key communicators for farmers.
- **Trainers and Facilitators:** Facilitators and trainers lead seminars, perform field demonstrations, and deliver training programs; they are vital communicators in assisting farmers in embracing new technology and methods.
- **Media Outlets:** Radio programs, television shows, and agricultural magazines that focus on farming and rural development serve as key communicators by providing valuable information and advice to rural audiences.
- **Agribusinesses and Input Suppliers:** Field officers and technical specialists are frequently employed by agribusinesses, seed firms, and agricultural input providers. Their role as vital communicators is to teach farmers about the appropriate use of inputs and technologies.
- **Local Educators and Schools:** Schools and educational institutions in rural areas, including agricultural schools, can serve as key communicators in educating students about modern agricultural practices, which they can then share with their families.

The successful transmission of information, the adoption of new practices, and the general improvement of agricultural and rural lives depend on effective contact with these important communicators. Important communicators play a crucial role in extension services by bridging the knowledge gap between local communities and experts. The quality and efficacy of communication processes are impacted by these phrases, which stand for important ideas in the field of communication. Below is a description of each:

1.15 Homophily

Homophily is defined as the tendency of individuals to identify with or find themselves drawn to those who have similar attributes, for example, age, gender, interests, background, or views. It may affect the choice of conversation partners and the degree of comfort during exchanges, which may have an impact on communication.

To establish a feeling of commonality, people frequently choose to speak with those who have similar interests or pursuits.

1.16 Heterophily

Heterophily is the inclination to interact or form relationships with people who are different from oneself. Heterophily can add a variety of viewpoints and experiences to communication, whereas homophily is centred on similarities.

An illustration of heterophilous communication in the workplace is when staff members from several departments work together on cross-functional initiatives and share ideas.

1.17 Credibility

Credibility in communication refers to the perceived trustworthiness, expertise, and reliability of the communicator. It greatly influences the receiver's willingness to accept and act on the information or message being conveyed.

Example: A medical doctor is considered a credible source of health information, and their recommendations are more likely to be trusted.

1.18 Fidelity

In communication, fidelity describes the degree of correctness and consistency with which a message or piece of information is sent or received. When a message is delivered with high fidelity, it is accurate; when it is transmitted with low fidelity, there may be distortions or inaccuracies.

For instance, in telecommunications, high-fidelity audio ensures precise sound reproduction, whereas low-fidelity audio can lead to distortion.

1.19 Empathy

Empathy is the capacity to comprehend and share the thoughts, emotions, and experiences of another individual. Developing rapport and emotional connection is an essential aspect of successful communication.

Example: An empathetic listener may identify with and feel the speaker's happiness or sorrow, which fosters a feeling of support and understanding.

1.20 Feedback

In communication, feedback is the information, responses, or feelings that are obtained from the recipient in response to a message. It enables changes and enhancements and offers insightful information on how well the communication worked.

Example: Following a presentation, the audience may provide feedback to the speaker, enabling them to better understand what went well and what needs to be improved for next time.

1.21 Communication Skills and Competence

These ideas influence how information is shared, interpreted, and used in communication. They are important components of communication dynamics. Understanding these elements can help people and organizations improve their communication tactics and create relationships that are more meaningful and productive. The ability to communicate effectively, comprehend others, and handle a variety of communication situations are all made possible by having strong communication skills and competency. They include a variety of skills and attributes that let people successfully communicate and share knowledge. An outline of communication competency and skills is provided below:

- **Communication Skills:** The capacity to actively and sympathetically hear someone out, understand what they're saying, and reply correctly. It takes skill to listen well to comprehend and establish rapport.
- **Verbal Communication**: is the ability to express information, ideas, and thoughts effectively and clearly through spoken words. Vocabulary, pronunciation, tone, and fluency are all included.
- **Nonverbal Communication:** refers to the ability to express ideas through body language, eye contact, gestures, and facial expressions. Verbal communication is frequently enhanced or reinforced by nonverbal signals.
- **Written Communication:** refers to the ability to convey concepts and details in written forms, like letters, essays, reports, and emails. Proficiency in writing guarantees professionalism and clarity.
- **Interpersonal Communication**: The ability to interact effectively in one-on-one or small- group settings. It involves building relationships managing conflicts, and fostering understanding.

- **Public:** Speaking in front of a bigger group of people with assurance and confidence is known as public speaking. Organization, delivery, and the capacity to enthral and fascinate an audience are all aspects of effective public speaking.
- **Cross-cultural Communication:** Proficiency in traversing cultural barriers to communication while taking into account variations in traditions, beliefs, and modes of communication is known as cross-cultural communication.
- **Digital Communication:** Proficiency in digital tools, platforms, and technology for communication, such as social media, video conferencing, email, and messaging applications, is a prerequisite for digital communication.

1.22 Communication Competence

- **Effectiveness:** The capacity to accomplish the planned communication goals is a sign of communication competence. Whether the goal is to inform, convince, educate, or promote understanding, effective communication produces the desired results.
- **Adaptability:** Skilled communicators can modify their methods depending on the audience, scenario, and environment. They are skilled at modifying their attitude according to the situation and know when to be formal or informal, forceful or sympathetic.
- **Clarity:** Competence is characterized by clear communication. It entails communicating ideas and concepts in a concise, and comprehensible way to minimize the possibility of misunderstanding.
- Successful communicators are skilled at both speaking and paying attention. They engage with speakers, ask questions, and make comments to ensure that everyone is understanding.
- **Active** Listening: Strong communicators are adept at both speaking and actively listening. To guarantee that everyone is comprehending, they interact with speakers, seek clarification, and offer comments.
- **Empathy:** Communicating with empathy indicates that one is sensitive to and understands the thoughts, feelings, and viewpoints of others. Trust and solid interpersonal ties are fostered by empathy.
- One of the most important aspects of competency is the capacity to resolve conflicts and disputes through communication. Competent

people know how to resolve conflicts in a way that benefits both parties.

- **Ethical Communication:** Maintaining moral values and standards like integrity, honesty, and respect is part of being a competent communicator. Communicating ethically increases credibility and trust.
- **Reception of Feedback:** Skilled communicators are receptive to feedback and willing to use it to further improve their skills. They understand that criticism is an important instrument for development and improvement.

Communication skills and competence are valuable in both personal and professional contexts. They contribute to effective collaboration, leadership, and the ability to convey messages, persuasively, and with impact. Developing and honing these skills and competencies can enhance an individual's overall communication effectiveness and success in various spheres of life.

1.23 Communication Models

1. Aristotle's Model of Communication The earliest model of communication was the symmetrical and simple model developed by the great Greek philosopher Aristotle. Aristotle in his model includes the five essential elements of communication, i.e., the speaker, the speech or message, the audience, the occasion, and the effect. In his rhetoric, Aristotle advises the speaker on constructing a speech for different audiences on different occasions for different effects. This model is most applicable to public speaking.

Aristotle Model of Communication

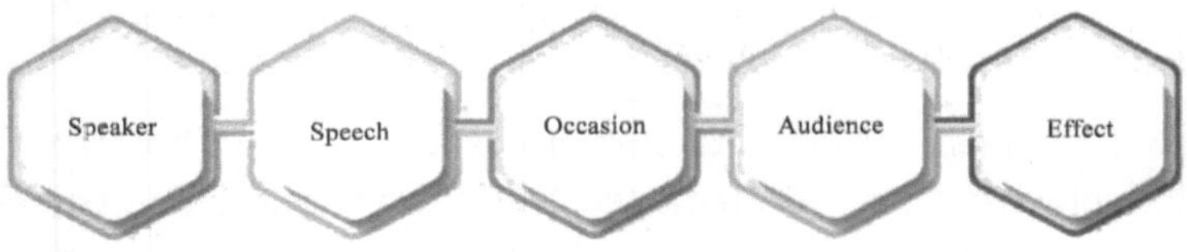

2. Shannon and Weaver model (1949) Shannon and Weaver's mathematical theory of communication (1949) is widely accepted as one of the main seeds out of which communication studies have grown. It is a clear example of the process school, seeing communication as the transmissions of messages. Shannon and Weaver's model (1949) presents communication as a linear process. As indicated by its name, the scholars believed that communication occurred in a linear fashion, where a sender encodes a message through a channel to a receiver, who will decode the message. Feedback is not immediate. Examples of linear communication were newspapers, radio, and television.

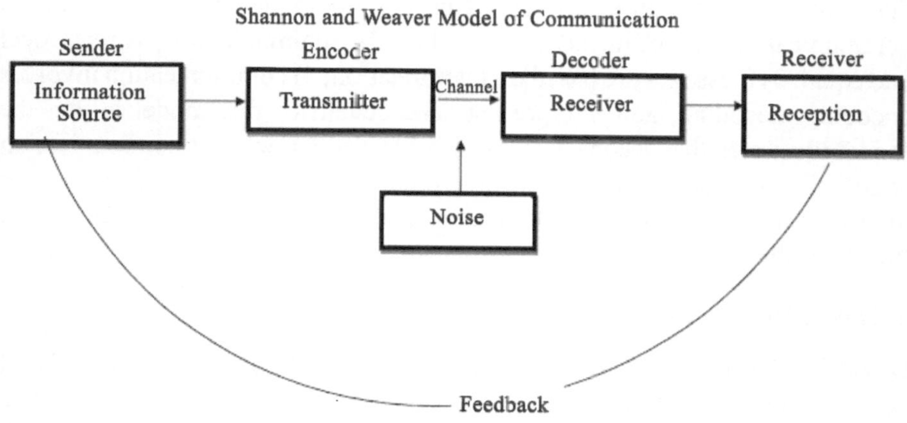

Source: www.busknowledgechauye.blogspot.com

As the diagram above indicates, this communication model comprises four elements. A source of information, with a greater or lesser number of messages to communicate; a transmitter or sender with the capacity to transform a message into a signal; a receiver which decodes the signal in order to retrieve the initial message, and finally, the destination, a person or thing for whom the message is intended. Communication, according to this model, follows a simple left to right process. The information source (say speaker), selects a desired message from all the possible messages. The message is sent through a transmitter (microphone) and is changed into signals. A receiver (say earphone), changed back into a message and given to the destination, a listener, receives the signals. In the process of transmission, certain distortions are added to the signal which are not part of the message and these will be called noise. The information source changes the message into the signal, which is actually sent over the communication channel from the transmitter to the receiver. In the process of being transmitted, usually certain things are added to the signal, which were not intended by the sender. These additions are distortion of sounds as in telephony, or static in radios, or errors in transmission in telegraphy or facsimile etc., Such changes in transmission signals are called noise.

3. C.E. Osgood - Schramm Model (1975) The Osgood-Schramm model is built on the theory that communication is a two-way street, with a sender and a receiver. Charles Egerton Osgood popularized the notion that communication was circular rather than linear, meaning that it required two participants taking turns sending and receiving a message. It indicates that messages can go in two directions. Hence, once a person decodes a message, then they can encode it and send a message back to the sender. They could continue encoding and decoding into a continuous cycle. This revised model indicates that: 1) communication is not linear, but circular; 2) communication is reciprocal and equal; 3) messages are based on interpretation; 4) communication involves encoding, decoding, and interpreting. The benefit of this model is that the model illustrates that feedback is cyclical. It also shows that communication is complex because it accounts for interpretation. This model also showcases the fact that we are active communicators, and we are active in interpreting the messages that we receive.

4. David Berlo's Model (1960)

David K. Berlo (1960) created the SMCR model of communication. SMCR stands for sender, message, channel, receiver. Berlo's model describes different components of the communication process. He argued that there are three main parts of all communication, which is the speaker, the subject, and the listener. He maintained that the listener determines the meaning of any message.

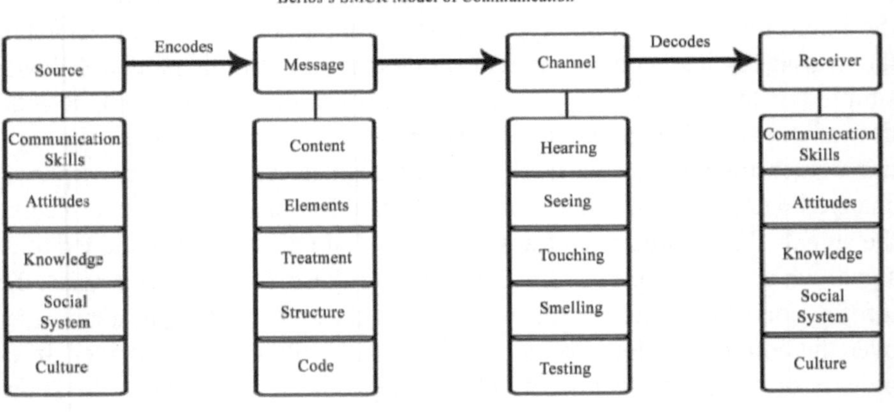

In regards to the source or sender of the message, Berlo identified factors that influence the source of the message. First, communication skills refer to the ability to speak or write. Second, attitude is the person's point-of-view, which may be influenced by the listener. The third is whether the source has requisite knowledge on a given topic to be effective. Fourth, social systems include the source's values, beliefs, and opinions, which may influence the message.

Next, we move onto the message portion of the model. The message can be sent in a variety of ways, such as text, video, speech. At the same time, there might be components that influence the message, such as content, which is the information being sent. Elements refer to the verbal and nonverbal behaviors of how the message is sent. Treatment refers to how the message was presented. The structure is how the message was organized. Code is the form in which the message was sent, such as text, gesture, or music.

The channel of the message relies on the basic five senses of sound, sight, touch, smell, and taste. Think of how your mother might express her love for you. She might hug you (touch) and say, "I love you" (sound), or make you your favorite dessert (taste). Each of these channels is a way to display affection.

The receiver is the person who decodes the message. Similar to the models discussed earlier, the receiver is at the end. However, Berlo argued that for the receiver to understand and comprehend the message, there must be similar factors to the sender. Hence, the source and the receiver have similar components. In the end, the receiver will have to decode the message and determine its meaning. Berlo tries to present the model of communication as simple as possible. His model accounts for variables that will obstruct the interpretation of the model.

1.24 Let's Evaluate

1. **What is the primary goal of communication in extension services?**

   a. To enforce regulations

   b. To control information

   c. To facilitate knowledge transfer and behavioural change

   d. To limit interactions

2. **In the context of extension services, why is effective communication important?**

   a. It simplifies the decision-making process for extension agents.

   b. It helps maintain secrecy and confidentiality.

   c. It enables knowledge dissemination, learning, and adoption of new practices.

   d. It minimizes the need for face-to-face interactions.

3. **Which of the following is NOT an essential component of effective communication in extension services?**
   a. Clear and concise messaging
   b. Empathy and understanding the audience's needs
   c. Exclusively using written communication
   d. Feedback and two-way communication
4. **When extension agents use homophily in their communication, what are they emphasizing?**
   a. The importance of diversity in their audience
   b. The value of open and inclusive communication
   c. Their similarity and shared interests with the target group
   d. The need for clear and concise language
5. **How does heterophily benefit extension services communication?**
   a. It creates a sense of common ground and shared experiences.
   b. It helps build trust and rapport with the audience.
   c. It introduces diverse perspectives and ideas.
   d. It limits the audience to a specific group.
6. **In extension services, what does "credibility" mean in the context of key communicators?**
   a. The ability to adapt to the audience's preferences
   b. The trustworthiness and expertise of the communicator
   c. The speed of message delivery
   d. The use of technical jargon
7. **What is the role of feedback in extension services communication?**
   a. To control and regulate the communication process
   b. To limit the flow of information from key communicators
   c. To assess the effectiveness of the communication and make necessary adjustments
   d. To introduce noise and distort the message

8. Why is adaptability important in communication competence in extension services?

a. To ensure messages are understood by all recipients

b. To maintain a rigid and unchanging communication style

c. To limit the scope of communication to a specific audience

d. To adjust communication based on the situation or audience's characteristics

9. Which aspect of communication competence in extension services is linked to respecting cultural norms and adjusting communication accordingly?

a. Effectiveness

b. Adaptability

c. Fidelity

d. Self-awareness

10. What does cognitive complexity in communication competence involve?

a. The ability to convey messages in multiple languages

b. The skill of using non-verbal communication effectively

c. Considering multiple and diverse perspectives when communicating

d. The practice of minimizing the use of non-verbal cues

11. Which of the following is not a characteristic of effective communication?

a. Clarity

b. Brevity

c. Complexity

d. Consistency

12. Communication is a two-way process. What are the two main components of this process?

a. Sender and receiver

b. Message and medium

c. Encoding and decoding

d. Noise and feedback

13. Which of the following is an example of non-verbal communication?

a. Speaking on the phone

b. Sending an email

c. Making eye contact

d. Writing a letter

14. Which type of communication occurs within a person, involving thoughts, perceptions, and self-talk?

a. Intrapersonal communication

b. Interpersonal communication

c. Mass communication

d. Organizational communication

15. When a manager communicates with employees to assign tasks and provide instructions, it is an example of:

a. Upward communication
b. Downward communication
c. Lateral communication
d. Diagonal communication

16. In a meeting, team members discuss ideas and share their thoughts openly. This is an example of:

a. Formal communication
b. Informal communication
c. Horizontal communication
d. Mass communication

17. What is the first step in the communication process?

a. Feedback
b. Encoding
c. Decoding
d. Noise

18. Which element of the communication process involves interpreting and making sense of the received message?

a. Encoding
b. Feedback
c. Decoding
d. Noise

19. When a receiver provides a response or reaction to a message, it is called

a. Encoding
b. Decoding
c. Feedback
d. Noise

20. What is the ability to understand and interpret non-verbal cues, such as body language and facial expressions known as?

a. Listening skills
b. Verbal communication
c. Non-verbal communication
d. Feedback

21. Which of the following is an example of an active listening skill?

a. Interrupting the speaker to share your own experiences

b. Making eye contact and nodding to show you are engaged

c. Avoiding eye contact to avoid distraction

d. Ignoring the speaker's emotions

22. Which communication skill involves the ability to express your thoughts, ideas, and feelings clearly and effectively?

a. Listening skills

b. Non-verbal communication

c. Verbal communication

d. Critical thinking

23. Communication competence is the ability to achieve effective communication. Which of the following is a component of communication competence?

a. Only focusing on your own message

b. Ignoring cultural differences

c. Adjusting your communication based on the situation and audience

d. Avoiding feedback from others

24. Which of the following is an essential aspect of intercultural communication competence?

a. Assuming that everyone shares the same cultural norms

b. Demonstrating respect for diverse cultural perspectives

c. Avoiding communication with people from different cultures

d. Stereotyping individuals based on their culture

25. What does emotional intelligence contribute to communication competence?

a. It hinders effective communication by making individuals overly emotional.

b. It helps individuals manage their emotions and understand the emotions of others.

c. It has no impact on communication competence.

d. It solely focuses on technical communication skills.

Answers

1. c. To facilitate knowledge transfer and behavioural change
2. c. It enables knowledge dissemination, learning, and adoption of new practices.
3. c. Exclusively using written communication
4. c. Their similarity and shared interests with the target group
5. c. It introduces diverse perspectives and ideas.
6. b. The trustworthiness and expertise of the communicator
7. c. To assess the effectiveness of the communication and make necessary adjustments
8. d. To adjust communication based on the situation or audience's characteristics
9. b. Adaptability
10. c. Considering multiple and diverse perspectives when communicating
11. c. Complexity
12. a. Sender and receiver
13. b. Making eye contact
14. a. Intrapersonal communication
15. b. Downward communication
16. b. Informal communication
17. a. Encoding
18. b. Decoding
19. c. Feedback
20. c. Non-verbal communication
21. b. Making eye contact and nodding to show you are engaged
22. c. Verbal communication
23. c. Adjusting your communication based on the situation and audience
24. b. Demonstrating respect for diverse cultural perspectives
25. b. It helps individuals manage their emotions and understand the emotions of others.

2

Media
and Development Communication

2.1 Audio-Visual Aids Classification

Audio-visual aids are tools that combine auditory and visual stimuli to facilitate learning and improve comprehension. They can make abstract ideas more concrete and understandable. Here's a classification of some commonly used audio-visual aids:

- **Audio Aids**

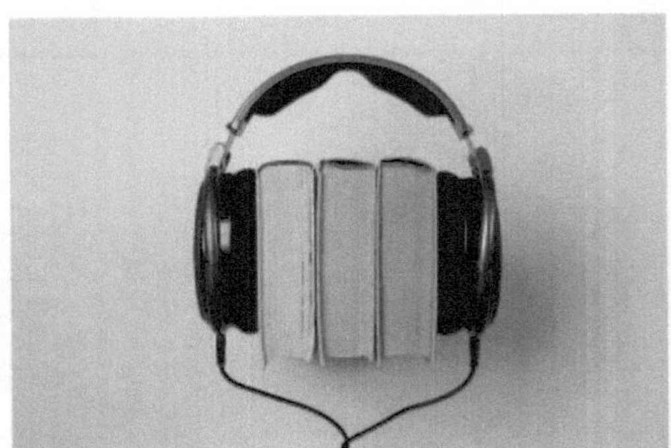

  - **Tape recorders:** are tools for teaching that playback sound or music.
  - **Radio:** Programmes can serve as educational resources and audio learning aids.
  - **Podcasts** are digital audio programs or episodes with a focus on learning.

- **Visual Aids**
  - **Charts and posters** are visual resources that are posted on a wall or a board.
  - **Flashcards:** Information-containing cards that are frequently used for memorizing.
  - **Photographs** are images that represent real- world situations, events, or objects.
  - **Maps:** Display geographical data.
  - **Diagrams** are condensed illustrations that describe an idea, procedure, or phenomenon.

  - **Flannel Boards:** Boards covered in flannel are used to stick characters or objects for storytelling.

- **Projection Equipment**
  - **Slide Projectors**: Devices that project images stored on transparent slides.

- **Overhead Projectors (OHP):** Devices that project transparent sheets onto a screen or wall.
- **Digital Projectors**: Devices that project digital images or videos from a computer onto a screen.
- **Film Projectors:** Devices used to project motion pictures.

- **Interactive Aids**
  - **Interactive Whiteboards (Smart Boards):** Touch-sensitive display boards connected to computers, allowing for interactive presentations.
  - **Tablets and Touchscreens:** Used for interactive learning applications.
- **Motion Aids**
  - **Videos and DVDs:** These can show processes, and historical events, or bring expert lectures to the classroom.
  - **Animations:** Animated sequences explaining complex topics in a visual and often simplified manner.
- **Models and Realia**
  - **Physical Models:** Three-dimensional representations of objects, organisms, or structures.
  - **Specimens:** Actual objects or materials (like rock samples, and plant parts) used in lessons.
  - **Dioramas:** Miniature representations of scenes.
- **Computer-based Aids**
  - **Educational Software:** Programs designed for instructional purposes.
  - **Simulations:** Computer-based models that imitate real-life processes or situations.

2.2 Selection of Audio-Visual Aids

When choosing which audio-visual aids to use, consider the following criteria:

- **Purpose of Instruction**: Understand the main goal of the lesson. Some topics might benefit more from videos, while others may need charts or diagrams.

- **Audience Characteristics:** Consider age, cultural background, prior knowledge, and other characteristics of the audience.
- **Availability of Equipment:** Ensure that the necessary equipment is available and in working condition.
- **Budget:** Some aids are more cost-intensive than others.
- **Ease of Use:** If the instructor is unfamiliar with certain technology, it might be better to choose more straightforward aids.
- **Size of the Audience:** Large groups might require projection equipment, while small groups could benefit from more hands-on aids like models.
- **Location and Setting**: A classroom may accommodate different aids compared to an open field or a small room.
- **Duration of the Lesson:** For shorter sessions, simple aids may suffice, but for longer, more detailed lessons, multimedia presentations might be more appropriate.
- **Feedback and Interaction:** If student interaction is desired, select interactive aids.
- **Relevance**: Ensure the aid is directly relevant to the lesson's content.

Using the right audio-visual aids can enhance the teaching-learning process, making content more engaging, relatable, and memorable for the audience.

2.3 Traditional Media

Traditional media is important for communication in extension and development, especially when it comes to rural and neglected regions. Traditional media channels are crucial for information transmission, capacity building, and community development since they are widely accessible in many rural areas where there is limited access to the internet and digital media. Here is an example of an extension using traditional media:

- **Radio Broadcasts:** Radio remains one of the most effective traditional media tools for extension services, especially in rural areas. Agricultural experts, extension workers, and local community members can broadcast agricultural advice, weather forecasts, market information, and development programs through radio. Radio broadcasts can be highly localized, allowing communities to access relevant information in their local dialects.
- **Television Programs:** Television can be used to reach a broader audience with instructional and educational programs related to agriculture, health, hygiene, and other development topics. Educational shows, documentaries, and talk shows can engage viewers and convey important information.
- **Print Materials:** Brochures, booklets, posters, and manuals are all examples of printed products that are useful for communicating in-depth information. You can hand out these papers during community gatherings, workshops, and training sessions. They act as resource manuals for farmers and rural areas.
- **Newspapers and Magazines:** Local newspapers and magazines often contain agricultural and rural development content. Articles, news, and advertisements provide a platform for sharing information on best practices, new technologies, and local events.
- **Community Meetings:** Face-to-face communication remains a powerful traditional extension method. Community meetings, gatherings, and events are used to discuss development initiatives, share experiences, and answer questions from community members.
- **Demonstrations and Field Days:** Live demonstrations and field days are a practical way to showcase new agricultural techniques, crop varieties, and best practices days and live demonstrations are useful ways to present cutting-edge farming methods, crop types, and best practices. Farmers can observe the outcomes and gain knowledge through practical application. Farmers can witness the results and learn through hands- on experience.
- **Local Language and Culture:** Traditional media takes into account local languages and cultural norms, ensuring that the communication is culturally sensitive and relevant to the community
- **Extension Workers and Agents:** Trained extension workers and agents are a form of traditional media themselves. They act as intermediaries, delivering information and knowledge directly to farmers and rural communities

- **Community Theatre and Storytelling:** Important lessons are communicated interestingly and enjoyably using storytelling and traditional theatre acts.
- **Direct Mail**: Mailed materials, such as newsletters and flyers, are sent to rural households to provide information on various topics, from health practices to agricultural techniques.

While digital and online media have gained prominence, especially in urban areas, traditional media remains a lifeline for rural extension and development. It bridges the digital divide and ensures that essential information reaches communities that may lack access to the internet. A combination of traditional and digital media can provide comprehensive extension services, catering to a wide range of audiences and addressing diverse communication needs.

2.4 Extension and Development Communication

• Concept

A specialized field called extension and development communication concentrates on sharing information and expertise to help rural, agricultural, and community development. The transfer of knowledge, technologies, and best practices to farmers, rural communities, and other stakeholders entails the strategic use of communication tools. Enhancing agricultural production, rural livelihoods, and overall socioeconomic development are the main objectives

• Importance

- **Agricultural Productivity:** For agricultural practices to be improved, which can raise food output and boost farmer income, extension and development communication is crucial.
- **Rural Development:** Effective communication plays a key role in the developmentofrural areas by promoting education, health, infrastructure, and other essential services.
- **Empowerment:** It gives rural people the knowledge and abilities necessary to make wise decisions regarding their farming methods and means of subsistence.
- **Innovation Adoption:** Communication helps in the adoption of innovative technologies and practices that can improve agricultural outcomes.

- **Market Access:** When rural producers are informed about market trends, demand, and pricing, they may reach markets more effectively.
- **Environmental Sustainability:** Communication can promote sustainable farming practices and environmental conservation.

- **Approaches**
  - **Face-to-Face Communication:** Through field trips, workshops, training sessions, and consultations, extension staff interact directly with farmers. This strategy enables personalized help and recommendations.
  - **Mass Media:** The use of mass media, including radio, television, and print materials, helps disseminate information to a broader audience. Radio, in particular, is a powerful tool in many rural areas.
  - **Community Meetings:** Organizing community meetings and gatherings provides a platform for sharing information and encouraging discussions among community members.
  - **Mobile and Digital Technology:** Communication for extension and development has become more and more dependent on mobile devices and digital platforms. Information can spread quickly and widely thanks to services like SMS messages, smartphone apps, and social media.
  - **Participatory Approaches:** Involving the community in decision-making and communication processes ensures that their needs and perspectives are considered.
  - **Training of Trainers (ToT):** Training residents to become "Trainers of Trainers" can have a multiplier effect on extending knowledge and abilities within a community.
  - **Demonstrations:** A powerful method of explaining complex ideas is through practical demonstrations of farming methods or technologies.
  - **Farmer Field Schools:** Farmers are encouraged to experiment with novel methods and practices through these participatory, group-based learning programs.
  - **Local Language and Culture:** Understanding regional languages and cultural norms is frequently necessary for effective communication to make sure the message is understood.

Feedback and Evaluation: The evaluation of communication efforts and ongoing feedback systems allow for continuous change strategies and content to the target audience's changing needs.

Extension and development communication is a dynamic field that evolves with the changing needs of rural communities and the development landscape. Its importance in supporting agricultural and rural development is underscored by its role in providing access to information, knowledge, and resources that can lead to improved living conditions and economic well-being in rural areas.

2.5 Organizational Communication

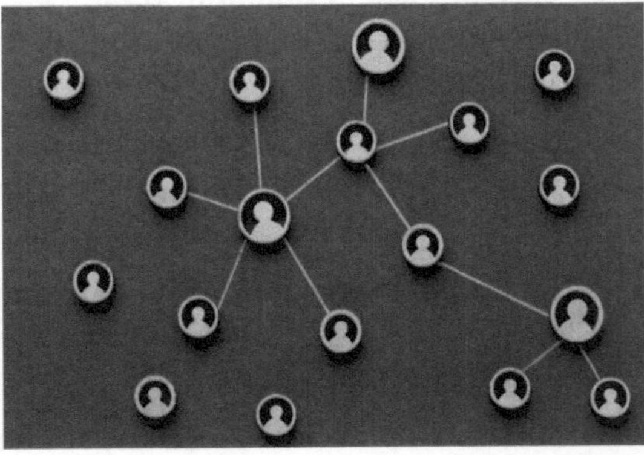

The exchange and flow of information among team members inside an organization is referred to as organizational communication. It covers a wide variety of contacts, including both formal documents and policies and unofficial conversations among team members. For smooth operations, cohesive teams, and overall productivity, an organization must have effective communication. Following is a breakdown:

Types of Organizational Communication

1. **Internal Communication: This refers to the communication that happens within the organization.**
2. **Upward Communication:** Feedback or reports from subordinates to managers.
3. **Downward Communication**: Instructions or policies disseminated from managers to subordinates.
4. **Horizontal Communication**: Communication between peers or employees at the same hierarchical level.
5. **External Communication:** Interaction that takes place between the organization and external entities like customers, suppliers, competitors, regulators, or the public.
6. **Formal Communication:** This refers to structured and official communication channels such as emails, memos, meetings, and reports

7. **Informal Communication**: Less organized channels, sometimes known as the "grapevine." Casual conversations, impromptu team lunches, or informal group chats are a few examples.

- **Importance of Organizational Communication**

1. **Facilitates Decision-making**: It makes sure information is communicated clearly and rapidly, promoting quick decision-making.
2. **Boosts Morale:** Employee morale might increase as a result of open and transparent communication since they feel appreciated and informed.
3. **Increases Productivity:** Effective communication lowers misconceptions, resulting in more efficient operations and higher production.
4. **Enhances Team Building:** Consistent communication promotes a sense of belonging, which improves team cohesion
5. **Manages and Implements Change:** Clear communication is essential to managing employee expectations and navigating transitions, particularly during times of organizational transformation.
6. **Establishes Transparency:** Open communication channels create an environment of trust and transparency.

- **Barriers to Effective Organizational Communication**

1. **Information Overload:** Having too much information might be just as bad as having too little. Employees could find it challenging to separate the important information from the surplus.
2. **Lack of Clarity**: Ambiguously framed messages can lead to misunderstandings.
4. **Hierarchical Barriers:** Organizational structures occasionally obstruct free communication, particularly in highly hierarchical settings.
5. **Physical Barriers**: Distances between departments or branches can challenge effective communication.
4. **Emotional Barriers:** Personal prejudices, emotions, or perceptions can distort the intended message.
5. **Cultural Differences:** Cultural misunderstandings can create difficulties in diverse workplaces.

- **Effective Organizational Communication Strategies**
    1. **Feedback Mechanisms:** Ensure there are outlets for feedback and a two-way exchange of information at all times.
    2. **Use of Technology:** Tools like intranets, corporate chat applications, and video conferencing can facilitate smoother communication.
    3. **Regular Training:** Training sessions on effective communication skills can be beneficial.
    4. **Open-door Policy:** Encourage a culture where employees feel they can approach management with concerns or ideas.
    5. **Clarity:** Make sure all communications, particularly instructions or policies, are explicit and clear.

Organizational communication is dynamic and should be continually assessed and adapted to meet the changing needs and challenges of an organization. Proper attention to it can lead to enhanced employee satisfaction, improved efficiency, and organizational success.

2.6 Modularized Communication

Modularized communication, often known as "modular communication," is a method of communication that divides complicated communications, material, or information into smaller, independent modules or components. Each module focuses on a certain feature or subject, and these modules can be combined, reorganized, or applied interchangeably to deliver a message or create a more thorough story. This strategy is particularly pertinent in a variety of industries and communication settings, such as education, technical documentation, content management, and software development. Following are some essential traits and uses of modularized communication:

Characteristics of Modularized Communication

- **Granularity**: Information is broken down into distinct modules that can be used separately or in combination to construct longer communication pieces.

- **Re-usability**: Modules are designed to be reusable in different contexts or across various communication materials.
- **Flexibility:** Modules can be mixed and altered to produce unique communication that is tailored to the audience's particular needs.
- **Scalability:** The approach accommodates the addition or removal of modules to adjust the level of detail or depth of communication.
- **Consistency:** Modular communication uses standardized modules to provide uniformity in messaging and material presentation.

Applications of Modularized Communication

- **Education**: In e-learning and instructional design, modularized content allows for flexibility in designing and delivering educational materials. It enables educators to adapt their teaching to different learning styles and student needs.
- **Technical Documentation**: In user manuals, product guides, and technical documentation, modularized content helps users access information efficiently. Users can focus on specific topics of interest or navigate the content at their own pace.
- **Content Management:** Content management systems (CMS) use modularized content to facilitate the creation, organization, and reuse of digital content on websites, blogs, and other online platforms.
- **Software Development**: In software development, modular programming breaks down software into small, manageable modules or functions. This makes code more organized, easier to maintain and simplifies debugging and updating.
- **Marketing and Advertising:** In marketing campaigns, modular communication allows marketers to create variations of content tailored to different target demographics, geographic regions, or products.
- **News and Journalism**: Modularized communication can be used in news articles to present information in a structured format, allowing readers to access specific sections or topics of interest.
- **Graphic Design**: In graphic design, modular layouts provide flexibility in designing print materials, websites, and other visual communication pieces.

- **Healthcare:** In healthcare communication, modularized content can be used for patient education materials, enabling healthcare professionals to select and customize information for individual patients.

Overall, modularized communication enhances flexibility and efficiency in delivering information. It empowers communicators to adapt their content for different audiences and purposes, making it a valuable approach in various professional fields and communication contexts.

Business communication is the process of communicating ideas and information with stakeholders outside of an organization as well as within one. To enable successful and efficient communication, it includes a variety of concepts, techniques, and procedures. An overview of principles, techniques, and procedures for business communication is provided below:

2.7 Concepts of Business Communication

- **Clarity**: To prevent misconceptions, effective communication demands straightforward language.
- **Conciseness:** Messages should be brief and to the point, without unnecessary information.
- **Audience-Centred:** Communication should consider the needs and perspectives of the audience.
- **Credibility:** Reliability and trustworthiness are crucial for successful business communication.
- **Feedback:** Encouraging feedback and two-way communication ensures that the message is understood and any concerns are addressed.
- **Formality:** The level of formality should match the context and audience, whether it's formal (e.g., reports) or informal (e.g., emails).

- **Active Listening:** Effective communication entails both speaking and paying attention to what others are saying.

Methods of Business Communication

- **Written Communication:** This includes emails, reports, memos, letters, and documentation.
- **Oral Communication:** Meetings, presentations, phone calls, and in-person conversations are all examples of verbal communication.
- **Visual Communication**: Charts, graphs, infographics, and presentations visually convey information.
- **Digital Communication**: Websites, instant messaging services, and social media are frequently utilized for business communication.
- **Non-verbal Communication:** Body language, facial expressions, and gestures can convey messages without words.
- **Interpersonal Communication**: Direct interactions between people are essential to building successful business connections.

Processes of Business Communication

- **Encoding:** The sender formulates the message and selects the most appropriate method to convey it.
- **Transmitting:** The message is sent through the chosen communication channel.
- **Receiving:** The recipient receives the message.
- **Decoding:** The recipient interprets the message, attempting to understand its meaning.
- **Feedback:** The recipient provides feedback to the sender, confirming comprehension or seeking clarification.
- **Noise:** Noise refers to any interference or barriers that can disrupt the communication process, such as distractions or technical issues.
- **Channel Selection:** Choosing the appropriate medium is crucial for successful communication.
- **Context:** Communication should consider the context and setting in which it occurs.
- **Audience Analysis:** Understanding the audience's background, needs, and preferences helps tailor the message.
- **Purpose:** The aim of communication, whether it is to inform, convince, or demand action, affects the approach and substance.

- **Organization**: Well-organized and structured messages are more effective.
- **Follow-up:** After communication, it's often necessary to follow up to ensure the message was received and acted upon.

Effective business communication involves the skilful application of these concepts, methods, and processes. It is vital for achieving organizational goals, resolving conflicts, building strong relationships, and making informed decisions. Additionally, technology and digital tools continue to shape the landscape of business communication, offering new methods and processes for more efficient and responsive interactions.

2.8 Use of Social Media in Communication

Social media plays a crucial role in modern communication, providing a platform for individuals, businesses, organizations, and governments to connect, share information, and engage with their target audience. Here are some key ways in which social media is used in communication:

1. **Information Dissemination**: Social media platforms are used to share news, updates, and information quickly and efficiently. News outlets, government agencies, and businesses use social media to provide real-time information to the public.
2. **Marketing and Promotion:** Businesses and brands use social media for marketing and promotion. They create and share content to reach a wider audience, build brand awareness, and engage with potential customers.
3. **Customer Engagement**: social media is a valuable tool for customer service and engagement. Companies can respond to customer inquiries, resolve issues, and gather feedback directly through social media channels.
4. **Public Relations:** Organizations use social media to manage their public image and reputation. They can address controversies, share positive news, and maintain open lines of communication with stakeholders.
5. **Community Building:** Social media platforms enable the creation of online communities and forums where people with shared interests

can connect and engage. These communities are often centred around hobbies, causes, or professional networks.

6. **Crisis Communication:** During emergencies or crises, social media can be used to convey critical information, provide safety instructions and reassure the public.
7. **Advocacy and Activism:** Activists and advocacy groups leverage social media to raise awareness, mobilize supporters, and advocate for social and political causes.
8. **Education and Training**: Educational institutions and professionals use social media to share educational content, connect with students and facilitate remote learning.
9. **Personal Expression**: Individuals use social media to express themselves, share their thoughts, experiences, and interests, and connect with friends and family.
10. **Collaboration and Networking:** Social media platforms facilitate professional networking, connecting individuals and businesses within specific industries or areas of interest.
11. **Event Promotion**: social media is a powerful tool for promoting events both online and in-person. Event organizers can create pages or events on social platforms, invite attendees, and provide updates.
12. **Influencer Marketing:** Brands partner with social media influencers to reach their followers and promote products or services.
13. **Political Communication:** Politicians and government entities use social media to communicate with constituents, share policy updates and engage in public discourse.
14. **Entertainment and Content Sharing**: social media is a hub for sharing multimedia content, such as videos, images, and music. It's a platform for artists, creators, and media companies to showcase their work.
15. **Global Reach:** social media transcends geographical boundaries enabling communication with a global audience. This is especially important for international businesses and global causes.
16. **Data Collection and Analysis:** Social media platforms generate a wealth of data that can be analysed to understand audience behaviour preferences, and trends, informing future communication strategies.

The impact and utility of social media in communication are vast and ever-evolving, making it a versatile and indispensable tool for individuals businesses, and organizations alike. However, the responsible and ethical use of social media is essential, considering factors such as privacy, security, and the potential for misinformation and fake news.

2.9 Media Mix

A media mix is a deliberate blend of diverse advertising and communication channels used to effectively reach a target audience. It encompasses both traditional (offline) and digital (online) media platforms, offering a comprehensive strategy for disseminating messages and achieving marketing objectives.

Traditional media channels such as television, radio, print (newspapers and magazines), and out- of-home advertising remain relevant, particularly for broad audience reach and brand visibility. On the other hand, digital media, including websites, social media, search engine marketing, and display advertising, offers precise targeting, interactivity, and real-time measurement.

The selection of media channels within the mix hinges on a deep understanding of the target audience, marketing goals, available budget, seasonality, and creative assets. Integration and consistency across all channels ensure a unified brand message. Regular assessment of the mix using data and key performance indicators (KPIs) allows for optimization and the refinement of advertising efforts.

In today's dynamic media landscape, the media mix serves as a versatile tool, accommodating evolving consumer behaviours and technologies. By harmoniously blending different media channels, businesses can craft impactful advertising campaigns that resonate with audiences and deliver measurable results.

2.10 Let's Evaluate

1. Which of the following is a characteristic of audio content?

a. Visual elements

b. Sound and images combined

c. Text-based information

d. Printed text

2. **Video content can be classified into various types. What category does a news report on television fall under?**

   a. Entertainment
   b. Educational
   c. Informational
   d. Fictional

3. **Which of the following is a traditional media platform?**

   a. Social media
   b. Television
   c. Podcasts
   d. Blogs

4. **In traditional media, what is the primary revenue source for newspapers and magazines?**

   a. Advertising
   b. Subscriptions
   c. Donations
   d. Government funding

5. **Which barrier to communication is characterized by the use of jargon or technical language that the receiver does not understand?**

   a. Noise
   b. Language barriers
   c. Cultural differences
   d. Selective perception

6. **When individuals make assumptions about what the other person means without seeking clarification, it is an example of which barrier to communication?**

   a. Noise
   b. Perception bias
   c. Language barriers
   d. Information overload

7. **What is the key advantage of modularized communication in a multimedia project?**

   a. It restricts creativity and flexibility.
   b. It simplifies the production process.
   c. It requires extensive technical skills.
   d. It eliminates the need for teamwork.

8. **In modularized communication, what does "modular" refer to?**

   a. A communication style that is rigid and linear
   b. Components that can be developed independently and combined to create a whole

c. A communication style that relies on one dominant speaker

d. A single, comprehensive communication channel

9. What type of content is most suitable for platforms like Instagram and Pinterest?

a. Long-form articles

b. Short tweets

10. Social media engagement metrics often include

a. Circulation numbers

b. Impressions and click-through rates

c. Visual content and images

d. Podcasts

c. Front-page headlines

d. Broadcast reach

11. What does the term "media mix" refer to in marketing and advertising?

a. A combination of various marketing tactics

b. The use of only one type of media for advertising

c. The exclusive use of social media for promotion

d. A technique used for graphic design

12. In a media mix strategy, why is it important to use a combination of different media types?

a. To save money on advertising costs

b. To reach a broader and more diverse audience

c. To focus all efforts on a single channel

d. To minimize the need for marketing research

13. Which element of the media mix is generally considered a traditional form of advertising?

a. Social media marketing

b. Content marketing

c. Print advertising

d. Influencer marketing

Answers

1) c. Text-based information
2) c. Informational
3) b. Television
4) a. Advertising
5) a. Language barriers
6) a. Perception bias
7) b. It simplifies the production process.
8) b. Components that can be developed independently and combined to create a whole
9) c. Visual content and images
10) b. Impressions and click-through rates
11) a. A combination of various marketing tactics
12) b. To reach a broader and more diverse audience
13) c. Print advertising

3

Understanding the Structure and Construction of News

3.1 Language and Principles of Writing: Basic Differences Between the Print, Electronic and Online News

Because each media has a unique readership with different needs, writing for print, electronic, and digital news demands distinct terminology and approaches. Here are the key differences:

Print News: Language

1. **Conciseness:** Print news requires concise and to-the-point writing due to limited space.
2. **Formal Language**: Language tends to be more formal and structured.
3. **Third Person:** Writing is often in the third person.
4. **Headlines:** Print headlines are shorter and must convey the essence of the story.
5. **Inverted Pyramid:** The inverted pyramid style, where the most important information comes first, is commonly used.

Principles

1. **Space Limitation:** Print news concentrates on the most important information due to physical space limitations.
2. **Editorial Control:** Editors have a significant role in deciding what gets published.
3. **Deadlines:** It's typical to have strict publication schedules with clear deadlines.
4. **Printed Permanence**: Once printed, it cannot be easily updated or corrected.
5. **Sequential Presentation:** Stories are presented linearly, with less multimedia integration.

Electronic News (TV and Radio): Language

1. **Oral Presentation:** The language is conversational and suitable for oral delivery.
2. **Sound and Visual Elements**: Emphasize the use of sound clips and pictures.
3. **Short and Catchy Phrases:** To evoke interest in the audience, use soundbites and catchphrases.
4. **Headlines and Teasers:** To promote news, headlines and teasers are commonly employed.
5. **Active Voice:** For immediacy, choose the active voice.

Principles

1. **Visual and Auditory Elements:** Places a focus on the utilization of images and sound to convey information.
2. **Speed and Immediacy:** Rapid delivery of breaking news is a goal of electronic news.
3. **Emotion and Engagement:** News is often intended to arouse emotions and keep viewers engaged.
4. **Interactivity:** Viewers or listeners may participate in real-time.
5. **Broadcast Schedule:** Adheres to a predetermined broadcast schedule, and news cycles are shortened.

Online News (Websites and Mobile Apps): Language

Web-Friendly Writing: Writing is optimized for online readability, with shorter paragraphs and more bullet points.

1. **Hyperlinks:** Makes use of hyperlinks to supply more data or references.
2. **Multimedia Integration:** Uses multimedia components such as infographics, movies, and pictures.
3. **Interactive Elements:** These may contain features that are interactive like comment sections or polls.
4. **User-Friendly Language:** Employs a user-friendly, informal tone.

Principles

1. **24/7 Availability:** Online news is accessible around the clock.
2. **Constant Updates:** As soon as new information becomes available; news can be updated instantly.
3. **User-Generated Content:** Encourages reader comments, user-generated content, and social media engagement.
4. **SEO and Metadata:** Increases discoverability through the use of search engine optimization (SEO) techniques.
5. **Diverse Platforms:** Tailors content for various devices and screen sizes.

These differences reflect the specific characteristics and expectations of each medium, emphasizing the need for journalists and writers to adapt their writing style and principles accordingly.

3.2 Organizing a News Story

To make sure that the information is presented to readers or viewers clearly and interestingly, a news item must be organized effectively. Journalism frequently employs the inverted pyramid structure, in which the most significant information is presented first and the details are offered in decreasing order of significance. An outline for constructing a news report is provided below.

1. **Determine the Key Information:** Identify the primary facts and details of the story. These should answer the 5Ws and 1H (Who, What, Where, When, why, and how).
2. **Write a Strong Lead:** The lead is the first line or paragraph that summarizes the most important information. It must grab the reader's interest and provide the core of the story. Usually, a strong lead comprises the who, what, where, and when.
3. **Develop the Body:** The body of the news story should provide additional details, background information, and context. Each paragraph should build upon the previous one, providing more information.
4. **Order of Importance:** Arrange the information in descending order of importance. This means that the most important details come first, followed by less critical information. This is where the inverted pyramid structure comes into play.
5. **Quotes and Attribution:** Use direct quotes from relevant sources to provide authenticity and humanize the story. Clearly attribute quotes and information to the sources.
6. **Background and Context:** Give background details so that the story gets context. Include any pertinent historical or statistical data when elaborating on the significance of the event or topic.
7. **Visual Elements:** Consider the use of visual elements like images, infographics, and videos to complement the text. Visuals can help convey the story more engagingly.
8. **Conclusion:** Summarize the story in the concluding paragraphs, bringing the reader back to the main point or highlighting any important takeaways.
9. **Additional Information:** Include any additional relevant information, such as contact details for sources or links to related articles or resources.
10. **Editing and Proofreading:** Make sure the news article is free of mistakes and grammatical errors by carefully editing and proofreading it.

11. **Headline and Subheadings:** Create a catchy headline that captures the core idea of the story. The story's body can be divided into sections for simpler comprehension by using subheadings.
12. **Byline and Date:** Include the byline (name of the author) and the publication date at the top of the story.
13. **Length Consideration:** Consider the length of the story. The most important information should be presented at the top of stories, which should be brief.
14. **Fact-Checking:** Ensure that the information is correct that has been provided. Make sure that all statements and claims are backed up by reliable sources. Always keep in mind that news writing requires brevity, accuracy, and clarity. Since readers frequently have limited time and attention, it is imperative to communicate the most significant information effectively and efficiently. The concept of the "5Ws and 1H" is fundamental in journalism and is a time-tested method for getting the full story on something. It's especially critical in news writing where brevity and clarity are essential. Each of the letters in this acronym represents a fundamental question that the reporter should aim to answer in the news story.

3.3 Here's a Breakdown of the 5Ws and 1H

- Who: Refers to the person or group involved in the story. It identifies the main subjects?

  Example: Who was involved in the accident?
- What: Details the event or occurrence.

  Example: What happened at the city council meeting?
- Where: Specifies the location of the event.

  Example: Where did the protest take place?
- When: Indicates the timing of the event.

  Example: When did the incident occur?
- Why: Explains the reasons, purposes, or causes behind the event.

  Example: Why did the mayor decide to resign?
- How: Describes the process or means by which something happened.

  Example: How did the firefighters tackle the blaze?

When organizing a news story using the 5Ws and 1H, it's typical to address the most critical elements (often the "Who," "What," "Where," and "When") in the lead or opening paragraph. This approach ensures readers immediately understand the crux of the story. The "Why" and "How" often require more elaboration and are delved into in subsequent paragraphs.

For example, a lead for a news story might read:

"A four-alarm fire broke out at the historic Main Street building in downtown Springfield earlier this morning, injuring three firefighters (Who & What). The blaze began around 5 a.m. (When) and quickly consumed the structure (How). Fire Chief John Doe believes an electrical short may have sparked the incident (Why)."

The story would then continue, delving deeper into each of these aspects, providing more details and context to the reader.

3.4 Inverted Pyramid Criteria for Newsworthiness

The inverted pyramid structure in news writing places the most newsworthy and essential information at the top of the story and follows with supporting details in descending order of importance.

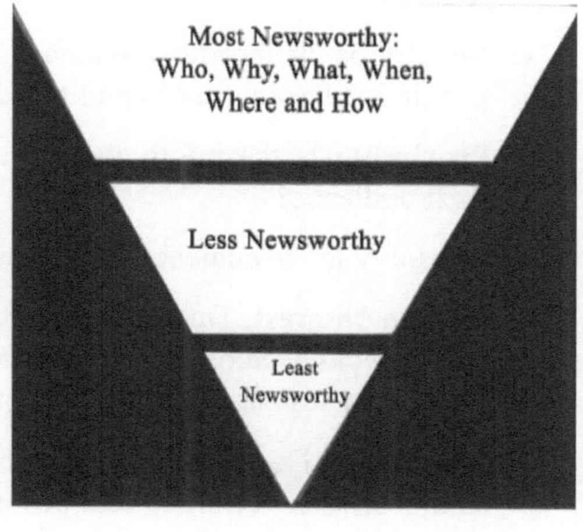

To determine the newsworthiness of information within the inverted pyramid structure, journalists consider several key criteria

- **Timeliness:** Is the information current and relevant to the target audience? Timely news is often more newsworthy. Events that have just occurred or are about to happen are usually at the top of the pyramid.
- **Significance:** Does the information have a significant impact on individuals, communities, or society at large? Stories that have a broad impact are more newsworthy.
- **Proximity:** Is the information geographically close to the audience or in a place of interest? Local news typically takes precedence over international news.

- **Prominence:** Does the information involve well-known individuals, organizations, or public figures? Stories involving prominent people or entities are often considered more newsworthy.
- **Conflict:** Does the information involve controversy, disagreement, or conflict?

  Conflicts and disputes can make a story more newsworthy due to the potential for significant impact.
- **Human Interest**: Does the story contain elements that resonate with human emotions or experiences? Human interest stories often engage readers due to their relatability and emotional content.
- **Currency:** Is the information fresh, providing updates on an ongoing situation or event? Current information can be more newsworthy due to its relevance.
- **Consequence:** Does the information have potential consequences, either positive or negative, for a wide audience? Stories with significant consequences are typically more newsworthy.
- **Novelty:** Is the information unique, unexpected, or surprising? Novelty and unusual events can capture readers' attention.
- **Proximity:** Is the information directly affecting or of interest to the local audience?

  Proximity to the audience can increase the newsworthiness of a story.
- **Human Interest**: Does the story connect with readers on a personal level, invoking emotions or experiences that are universally understood? Human interest stories often have broad appeal.
- **Magnitude:** Does the information concern a large-scale event, such as a natural disaster or a significant government decision? Stories with a high magnitude are considered more newsworthy.

Journalists use these criteria to determine the order of importance of the information they include in a news story. The most newsworthy elements, often related to the 5Ws and 1H (Who, what, Where, When, why, and how), are placed at the beginning of the story, ensuring that readers quickly grasp the essential aspects of the news.

3.5 Principles of News Selection

The principles of news selection, also known as news values or news criteria, guide journalists in deciding which stories to cover and prioritize. These principles help ensure that news organizations provide their audiences with the most relevant, impactful, and informative stories. Common news selection principles include:

- **Timeliness:** Stories that are current, recent, or about to happen are prioritized. Timely news is often at the forefront because it is considered the most relevant to readers and viewers.
- **Significance:** News stories with a significant impact on individuals, communities, or society at large are prioritized. This includes stories about major policy changes, natural disasters, or significant cultural events.
- **Prominence:** News involving well-known individuals, public figures, or organizations often takes precedence. People are interested in the activities and actions of prominent figures.
- **Proximity:** Stories that are geographically close to the audience or in places of interest to the audience receive priority. Local news is generally considered more relevant than international news.
- **Conflict/Controversy:** Stories involving conflict, disputes, or controversy capture attention due to their potential impact and the inherent drama they present.
- **Human Interest:** Stories that appeal to readers' emotions, experiences and relatability are prioritized. Human interest stories often engage readers on a personal level.
- **Currency:** News that provides updates on ongoing situations or evolving events is considered more newsworthy because it maintains the audience's interest.
- **Consequence:** Stories that have significant consequences, either positive or negative, for a wide audience are prioritized. This includes stories about policy decisions, economic trends, and environmental issues.
- **Novelty:** Unique, unexpected, or surprising stories are more newsworthy. Unusual events or discoveries capture attention.
- **Magnitude:** News that concerns large-scale events, such as natural disasters, major scientific breakthroughs, or significant political changes is often prioritized.
- **Rarity**: Stories about rare or uncommon occurrences may be considered newsworthy due to their uniqueness.

- **Conflict with Norms:** News that challenges or deviates from societal norms, values, or expectations may be considered newsworthy.
- **Human Rights and Ethics:** Stories related to violations of human rights or ethical issues often have high news value due to their moral and societal significance.
- **Relevance to Target Audience**: News organizations prioritize stories that are relevant to their target audience. This involves considering the interests, concerns, and demographics of the readers or viewers.
- **Balance and Diversity:** A mix of different types of news is important. News organizations aim for a balanced mix of local, national, international, hard news, soft news, and feature stories to cater to a wide range of interests.

These principles guide journalists in making editorial decisions about what stories to cover and how to present them to their audiences. The specific weighting of these principles may vary depending on the editorial focus and mission of the news organization.

3.6 Use of Archives, Sources of News, Use of Internet

Archives and the internet are two significant sources of information for news organizations. Both have their specific advantages, and their use depends on the nature of the news story being pursued. Let's delve into the uses, advantages, and limitations of each:

Archives as a Source of News

- **Historical Context:** Archives include past information that can provide depth to the context of news articles today. Journalists can provide a greater knowledge of a topic by drawing parallels between occurrences from the past and the present.
- **Verification:** Archives can serve as a fact-checking tool. For old events or statements made by public figures in the past, journalists can refer to archives to ensure accuracy.

- **Anniversaries & Commemorations:** On their anniversaries, significant historical events are frequently reexamined, and archives provide the necessary details.
- **Follow-ups:** For ongoing stories or issues, archives provide the background necessary for follow-up articles.
- **Source Material:** Documents, images, and videos from the past can be utilized to support present stories.

Limitations of Archives

Archives might not always be digitized or easily accessible.

There could be gaps in archived information or issues with the preservation of material.

Internet as a Source of News

- **Real-time Updates:** The internet, especially social media, offers real-time updates on developing stories.
- **Diverse Sources:** Journalists have access to a variety of sources, including government websites, academic portals, blogs, and discussion boards.
- **Global Reach:** The internet allows journalists to research and report on events from around the world without physically being there.
- **Interactivity:** Journalists can engage with sources and audiences directly, soliciting feedback, or user-generated content.
- **Multimedia Capabilities:** The internet supports multimedia elements, enhancing storytelling with videos, infographics, and interactive content.
- **Search Capabilities:** Search engines enable journalists to find specific information quickly.

Limitations of the Internet

The accuracy of online information can vary; there's a lot of misinformation and unverified content.

3.7 Let's Evaluate

1. **What is the traditional structure of a news story, often referred to as the "inverted pyramid"?**
   a. It starts with a summary and ends with the most important details.
   b. It begins with the most important details and progresses to less significant information.
   c. It organizes information in a circular pattern.
   d. It follows a chronological sequence.
2. **In a news story, the "lead" is also known as**
   a. The conclusion
   b. The headline
   c. The introduction
   d. The body
3. **Which writing style is commonly associated with news writing and emphasizes brevity and clarity?**
   a. Academic style
   b. Literary style
   c. Inverted style
   d. News style
4. **Which of the following is a fundamental principle of news writing that emphasizes objectivity and impartiality?**
   a. Sensationalism
   b. Advocacy
   c. Fairness
   d. Editorialization
5. **Which medium is best known for its immediacy and ability to provide real-time news updates?**
   a. Print
   b. Electronic
   c. Online
   d. Digital
6. **In print news, what is often a key consideration due to space limitations?**
   a. Visual elements
   b. Hyperlinks
   c. Word count
   d. Interactivity
7. **What is the main purpose of the "nut graph" in a news story?**
   a. To introduce the main characters
   b. To provide a concise summary of the story's main point

c. To offer a humorous anecdote

d. To describe the story's setting in detail

8. When selecting news stories for publication or broadcast, which of the following factors is a priority for many news organizations?

a. Personal preferences of the journalists

b. Profit potential

c. Length of the story

d. Entertainment value

9. What is the role of news archives in journalism?

a. To store current news stories

b. To provide historical context and access to past news articles

c. To promote advertising revenue

d. To keep track of journalists' personal work records

10. Which of the following is an example of a primary source in journalism?

a. A press release issued by a company

b. An opinion piece written by a journalist

c. A report summarizing a research study

d. An interview with a witness to an event

11. How has the internet changed the landscape of journalism?

a. It has decreased the speed of news dissemination.

b. It has reduced the availability of diverse news sources.

c. It has enabled citizen journalism and interactive storytelling.

d. It has eliminated the need for professional journalists.

Answers

1. b. It begins with the most important details and progresses to less significant information.
2. c. The introduction
3. d. News style
4. c. Fairness

5. c. Online
6. c. Word count
7. b. To provide a concise summary of the story's main point
8. b. Profit potential
9. b. To provide historical context and access to past news articles
10. a. A press release issued by a company
11. c. It has enabled citizen journalism and interactive storytelling.

4

Journalism

4.1 The Meaning of Journalism

The profession and practice of journalism entail gathering, confirming, analysing, and distributing news and information to the general public. Reporters, often known as journalists, are essential to the accurate, timely, and insightful coverage of events, problems, and advancements that have an impact on society. They are responsible for presenting the facts, providing diverse viewpoints, and conveying information in a clear, objective, and ethical manner.

4.2 Scope of journalism

The scope of journalism is broad and diverse, encompassing various forms of media and areas of coverage. Here are some key aspects of the scope of journalism:

1. **News Beats:** A variety of media platforms, such as print (newspapers and magazines), broadcast (television and radio), online news portals, social media, and multimedia formats, are used to practice journalism. Each platform offers unique opportunities and challenges for journalism.
2. **Investigative Journalism** reveals hidden facts, exposes corruption, and holds people, groups, or governments responsible through in-depth investigation and reporting. Journalists who conduct investigations frequently work on extended assignments.
3. **Features and Human-Interest Stories:** Journalism offers more in-depth looks at the lives and experiences of people and communities, besides hard news. Features and human-interest pieces fall under this category.
4. **Opinion and Editorial Writing:** Journalists may write opinion pieces and editorials to express their views and insights on current events and issues. These pieces are often labelled as such to distinguish them from objective news reporting.
5. **Photojournalism:** Photographers use visual images, primarily photographs, to tell news stories and convey information. Visual reporting is a powerful and impactful form of journalism.

6. **Broadcast Journalism** Broadcast journalists work on television and radio delivering news reports and stories through spoken words and visual or audio elements. This field includes anchors, correspondents, and producers.

7. **Online and Digital Journalism:** The digital age has expanded the scope of journalism to include online news websites, blogs, podcasts, and social media reporting. Digital journalists often use multimedia elements and engage with audiences in real-time.

4.3 Importance of Journalism

Journalism is of paramount importance in society for several reasons:

1. **Informing the Public**: Journalism provides the public with accurate, up-to-date information about local, national, and global events, allowing citizens to make informed decisions and participate in civic life.
2. **Check on Power:** Journalists act as watchdogs by monitoring government activities, exposing corruption and abuse of power, and holding institutions and public officials accountable.
3. **Fostering Transparency:** Journalism promotes government transparency and accountability, ensuring that actions and decisions are open to public scrutiny.
4. **Promoting Accountability**: Through investigative reporting and public interest stories, journalism encourages accountability in both the public and private sectors.
5. **Public Discourse:** Journalism fosters public discourse by providing a platform for diverse viewpoints and discussions on social, political, and economic issues.
6. **Crisis Reporting:** During crises, such as natural disasters, public health emergencies, and conflicts, journalism plays a crucial role in delivering emergency information and facilitating public safety.
7. **Preservation of History:** Journalism documents and preserves historical events and societal changes, creating an essential archive for future generations.

8. **Entertainment and Culture:** Journalism includes coverage of cultural events, entertainment, and sports, contributing to the cultural fabric of society.
9. **Community Engagement:** Local journalism, in particular, plays a vital role in informing and engaging communities, covering issues that directly affect residents.

Overall, journalism is a cornerstone of democracy, promoting transparency, accountability, and the public's right to know. It serves as a vital bridge between government, institutions, and the public, fostering an informed and engaged citizenry.

4.4 Principles of Journalism

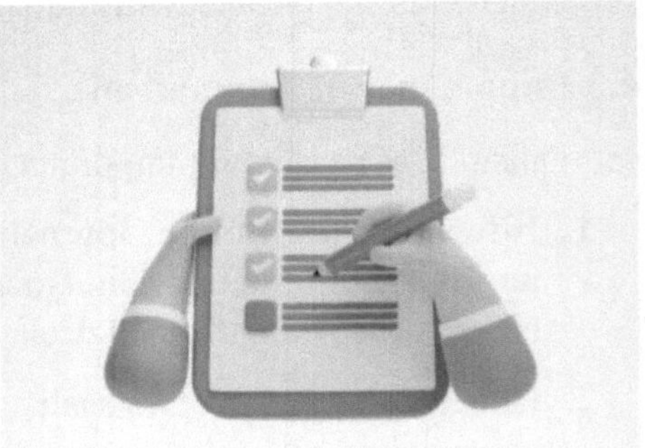

Journalism operates on a set of core principles that guide journalists in their work, ensuring that the news they produce is reliable, accurate, and serves the public interest. These principles uphold the integrity of journalism and help maintain public trust in the media. Here are the fundamental principles of journalism:

- **Truth and Accuracy:** Journalists have an obligation to report the facts and strive for accuracy in all they do. Ensuring information is correct is essential to building credibility.
- **Independence:** Journalists must act independently and free from influence, whether from advertisers, stakeholders, or political entities. Their primary commitment should be to the public.
- **Fairness and Impartiality:** Journalists should give a fair and balanced view of events. They should represent different viewpoints and interests without bias.
- **Humanity:** Journalists should always consider the impact of their reporting on people's lives and avoid causing harm, whether physical, psychological, or emotional.
- **Accountability:** Journalists must take responsibility for their work and be ready to correct any errors. Being transparent and accountable helps maintain the trust of the public.

- **Transparency:** Journalists should clearly differentiate between facts, opinions, and commentary. They should also be transparent about their sources and the method of gathering information.
- **Right to Privacy:** Everyone has a right to privacy. Journalists should ensure that they don't intrude on private lives unless there's a clear public interest.
- **Protection of Sources:** Sometimes, sources may only be willing to provide information under conditions of anonymity. Journalists should respect and protect these sources to maintain trust and the flow of information.
- **Avoid Conflicts of Interest:** Whether financial or personal, conflicts of interest can compromise the integrity of journalism. Journalists should declare any potential conflicts and, when possible, avoid them.
- **Minimize Harm:** Especially relevant when reporting on sensitive issues or vulnerable groups, journalists should strive to minimize harm. They should display compassion, sensitivity, and respect for their subjects.
- **Fact-check and verify:** In the age of instant information and the spread of misinformation, journalists should always verify facts from multiple credible sources before publishing.
- **Access and Openness:** Journalists should champion the public's right to information and push for open access to sources, especially in government and public institutions.
- **Commitment to Justice:** Journalists should avoid any form of discrimination in their reporting and be committed to social justice, ensuring that marginalized voices are heard.

These principles of journalism serve as an ethical framework for journalists worldwide, guiding them in their duty to provide the public with information that is fair, accurate, and relevant. It is essential for journalists to uphold these principles to maintain the credibility of the media and the trust of the public.

4.5 Journalism Theory

Journalism theories are frameworks that help explain and understand the practice of journalism, the role of media in society, and the impact of news on the public. These theories offer insights into how journalism functions and its effects on individuals and communities. Here are some key theories of journalism:

- **Gatekeeping Theory:** This theory focuses on the role of media gatekeepers, such as editors and news directors, in deciding what news gets published or broadcast. Gatekeepers select and priorities stories based on their judgement of newsworthiness, which can influence the public's agenda and perception.
- **Agenda-Setting Theory:** Agenda-setting theory suggests that the media doesn't tell people what to think but rather what to think about. Media coverage can shape public priorities and issues by highlighting certain topics over others.
- **Framing Theory:** Framing theory explores how the media can frame or present news stories in specific ways to influence public perception. Journalists can frame stories to emphasize certain aspects or themes, affecting how the audience interprets the information.
- **Cultivation Theory:** Cultivation theory posits that long-term exposure to certain media content can shape an individual's perception of reality. It suggests that heavy consumption of media can lead to a distorted view of the world based on media portrayals.
- **Spiral of Silence Theory:** The spiral of silence theory describes how people tend to withhold their opinions or conform to perceived majority views due to a fear of isolation or backlash. It can influence public discourse and the information that individuals choose to share or consume.
- **Two-Step Flow Theory:** This theory argues that media influence's opinion leaders first, and those opinion leaders, in turn, influence their peers. It challenges the direct effects model, suggesting that media influence is mediated by personal interactions.
- **Agenda-Building Theory:** The agenda-building theory extends the agenda- setting theory by emphasizing the role of different stakeholders, including the public and interest groups, in influencing media coverage. It acknowledges that the media can both set and respond to the public agenda.
- **Media Effects Theories**: Media effects theories, such as the cultivation theory and the reinforcement theory, explore how media can influence attitudes, beliefs, and behaviours. These theories examine the potential impact of media on individuals and society.

- **Diffusion of Innovations Theory:** This theory is concerned with the social diffusion of innovations, new ideas, and technologies. When journalists inform the public about inventions, they frequently contribute to the dissemination process.
- **Participatory Journalism and Citizen Journalism:** These theories address the evolving role of the audience in journalism. Participatory journalism emphasizes audience engagement and interaction with news content, while citizen journalism involves non-professionals contributing to news reporting.
- **The Public Journalism Movement:** Public journalism advocates for a more active and participatory role for the public in shaping news agendas and decision- making. It aims to enhance civic engagement and public discourse.
- **Digital Media Theories:** The advent of digital media has given rise to theories like the digital divide, which examines disparities in access to online information, and networked journalism, which explores the impact of digital technologies on news production and distribution.

These journalism theories offer valuable frameworks for understanding the complex relationship between media, society, and individuals. They provide insights into how news is produced and consumed and its effects on public opinion and behaviour.

4.6 Growth Factors for Farm Journalism

- **Technological Advancements**: The growth of digital technology, including the internet and social media, has created new opportunities for farm journalism. Agricultural journalists can reach a broader audience, share information in real time, and engage with readers more interactively.
- **Agricultural Innovations:** The agriculture sector has witnessed significant advancements in technology, sustainable farming practices, and agribusiness. Farm journalism has the opportunity to showcase these innovations and educate farmers about modern techniques and tools.

- **Global Food Security and Sustainability:** Agriculture has been receiving attention due to concerns about sustainability and food security. Through the promotion of ethical and sustainable practices in agriculture, farm journalism may address these important challenges.
- **Rural Development and Policy:** Rural areas and agriculture often play a vital role in a country's economic development. Farm journalism can inform policymakers, farmers, and the public about rural development initiatives, government policies, and their impact on farming communities.
- **Market Trends and Trade:** As global markets become more interconnected, farm journalism can help farmers understand market trends, export opportunities, and international trade policies that affect their livelihoods.

4.7 Challenges Facing Farm Journalism

Economic viability: Many traditional media outlets, including newspapers and magazines, have faced economic challenges. This has led to the downsizing or closure of dedicated agricultural sections, impacting the resources available for farm journalism.

- **Changing Media Landscape:** The shift to digital media has disrupted traditional journalism models. Farm journalists must adapt to the changing landscape and find sustainable ways to reach their audience online.
- **Diverse Audience:** Farmers are a diverse group with varying information needs.

  Effective farm journalism must cater to different segments of the farming community, from small-scale farmers to large commercial operations.
- **Access to Information:** In some rural areas, limited internet access and digital literacy can pose challenges for farmers to access online agricultural information. Farm journalists need to consider these accessibility issues.
- **Farmers' Trust:** Building and maintaining trust with the agricultural community is crucial for farm journalism. This trust can be eroded if journalists are seen as disconnected from farming realities or influenced by external interests.
- **Sensitivity to Local Issues**: Farm journalism must take into account local and regional agricultural issues, as farming practices and challenges can vary widely by location.

- **Environmental Concerns:** The environmental impact of the agriculture industry is being examined more and more. Sustainable practices should be promoted, and these issues should be covered fairly in farm journalism.
- **Support of Young Farmers:** The future of agriculture depends on the support of the farming community. The difficulties and opportunities faced by young farmers can be brought to light by agricultural journalism.

In conclusion, the growth of farm journalism is closely tied to technological advancements, agricultural innovations, and the increasing importance of sustainability and food security. However, the field faces challenges related to economic sustainability, the changing media landscape, diverse audience needs, and the need for trustworthy, locally relevant information. For farm journalism to flourish further, it is essential to address accessibility difficulties, adapt to new media technology, and preserve the trust of the agricultural community.

4.8 Let's Evaluate

1. **What is the primary purpose of journalism?**
   a. To entertain the audience
   b. To promote political ideologies
   c. To provide timely and accurate information to the public
   d. To sell products and services
2. **In journalism, the term "beat" refers to**
   a. A rhythmic pattern in news reporting
   b. A specific area or topic of news coverage
   c. A popular headline format
   d. A type of photojournalism technique
3. **Why is journalism often referred to as the "Fourth Estate" in democratic societies?**
   a. Because it has four main sections: politics, economy, culture, and sports
   b. Because it is not influenced by any external factors

c. Because it plays a critical role in checking and balancing government power

d. Because it is focused on entertainment and leisure

4. Which of the following is a key role of journalism in society?

a. To promote sensationalism and tabloid news b. To manipulate public opinion

c. To inform citizens, hold institutions accountable, and foster transparency

d. To avoid critical reporting and maintain a harmonious society

5. Which journalistic principle emphasizes presenting multiple perspectives on a given issue to achieve balance and fairness?

a. Objectivity

b. Sensationalism

c. Advocacy

d. Editorialization

6. Which journalism theory asserts that the media has the power to shape public perception and influence societal norms?

a. The Agenda-Setting Theory

b. The Libertarian Theory

c. The Cultivation Theory

d. The Uses and Gratifications Theory

7. What factor contributes to the growth of farm journalism?

a. Urbanization and the decline of agriculture

b. Increased specialization in farming practices

c. A lack of technological advancements in agriculture

d. Reduced access to information in rural areas

8. What is a common challenge faced by farm journalism in the digital age?

a. Lack of interest in agricultural topics

b. Decreased accessibility to information

c. Competition from social media and online platforms

d. The abundance of traditional print publications

9. Environmental issues and sustainability concerns in agriculture fall under which challenge for farm journalism?

a. Technological challenges

b. Economic challenges

c. Socio-political challenges

d. Content and thematic challenge

Answers

1. c. To provide timely and accurate information to the public
2. b. A specific area or topic of news coverage
3. c. Because it plays a critical role in checking and balancing government power
4. c. To inform citizens, hold institutions accountable, and foster transparency
5. a. Objectivity
6. c. The Cultivation Theory
7. b. Increased specialization in farming practices
8. c. Competition from social media and online platforms
9. d. Content and thematic challenges

5

Facets of Journalism

5.1 Basics of Writing

Writing news stories involves a specific set of guidelines and practices to ensure accuracy, clarity, and effective communication.

- **Writing News Stories**

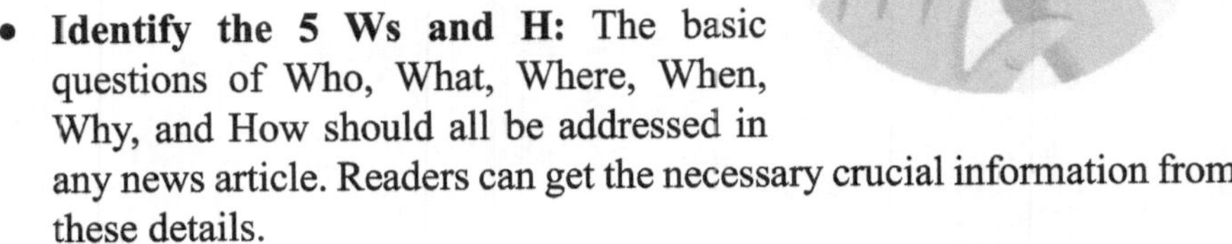

A methodical approach is necessary when writing news articles in order to provide accurate, educational, and captivating information.

The following are fundamentals of news story writing:

- **Identify the 5 Ws and H:** The basic questions of Who, What, Where, When, Why, and How should all be addressed in any news article. Readers can get the necessary crucial information from these details.
- **Start with a Strong Headline:** The headline should be concise, attention-grabbing, and summarize the main point of the story.
- **Write a Compelling Lead:** The lead, which is the first paragraph, should contain the most important details. Usually, it provides the most significant Ws and H replies.
- **Follow the Inverted Pyramid Structure:** Sort the information according to decreasing priority. Go step-by-step from the most important information to the less important aspects.
- **Use the Active Voice:** Write in the active voice for clarity and conciseness. Passive voice can make sentences more complex.
- **Avoid Jargon and Technical Terms:** Write in language that is easy to understand for a wide range of readers.
- **Provide Quotes and Attribution:** When quoting sources, attribute the statements to their sources and provide context for the quotes.
- **Check Facts and Verify Information:** Verify facts and details with trustworthy sources to ensure the accuracy of the material.
- **Edit and Proofread:** Carefully review your story for grammar, spelling, and punctuation errors. Also, check for clarity and consistency.

- **Include Relevant Background:** Provide context or background information if needed in the story to aid readers in understanding the subject.
- **Use Associated Press (AP) Style:** Following a widely accepted style guide like AP Style helps maintain consistency in writing and formatting.
- **Engage the Reader:** Make the story captivating by using storytelling strategies and descriptive language.
- **Avoid Bias:** Maintain objectivity and report the facts without expressing personal opinions or biases.
- **Cite Sources and Data:** If you use statistics or data, provide the source or reference for credibility.
- **Include Visual Elements:** Whenever necessary, enrich the story with pertinent photos, videos, or graphics.
- **Be Timely:** Publish news stories as close to the event or development as possible to maintain relevance.
- **Consider the Target Audience:** Whether your target is a broad readership, a particular industry, or a local community, you ought to customize your writing to suit their requirements and interests.
- **Use Quotation Marks for Direct Speech:** When you directly quote someone, enclose the uttered words in quotation marks.
- **Attribution for Claims and Assertions:** Whenever a claim or assertion is made, give due credit to the relevant authority or source.

Recall that providing accurate and unbiased information is the goal of news writing. Whether it's hard news, feature, or editorial writing, the structure and style may change, but the principles of concise, clear, and informative writing always apply.

- **Writing Feature Articles**

Writing feature articles, unlike news reporting, allows for more creative storytelling and exploration of various subjects. Feature articles often delve into human interest, provide in-depth analysis, and engage readers emotionally. Here are the basics of writing feature articles:

- **Select a Compelling Topic:** Choose a topic that is interesting, unique, and relevant to your target audience. Feature articles can cover a wide range of subjects, from profiles of individuals to in-depth explorations of trends or events.

- **Research Thoroughly:** Conduct comprehensive research to gather facts, statistics, and background information. This will provide substance and credibility to your article.
- **Angle and Focus:** Determine a specific angle or focus for your feature. What aspect of the topic will you explore? What's the central theme or message?
- **Structure:** Unlike news stories, feature articles don't follow the inverted pyramid structure. They often start with a hook or an anecdote to draw readers in and then unfold the narrative, providing context and details before reaching the main point.
- **Engaging Lead:** Craft an engaging lead that piques the reader's curiosity and sets the tone for the rest of the article. It could be a captivating story, a thought-provoking question, or a surprising fact.
- **Narrative and Storytelling:** Feature articles often rely on storytelling techniques. Use anecdotes, personal experiences, and dialogue to make the story relatable and engaging.
- **Quotes and Anecdotes:** Include relevant quotes and anecdotes from people connected to the topic. These add authenticity and human interest to the story.
- **Descriptive Writing:** Use descriptive language to paint a vivid picture for the reader. Engage the senses and create a sensory experience.
- **Incorporate Research and Statistics:** While storytelling is essential, include relevant research, statistics, and expert opinions to support your claims.
- **Structure and Subheadings:** Break up the article into sections or subheadings to make it more scannable and easier to navigate.
- **Voice and Style:** Develop a unique writing voice and style that suits the topic and audience. This can include being conversational, formal, humorous, or reflective.

- **Audience Awareness:** Keep your target audience in mind. Tailor the tone, language, and examples to match their interests and knowledge level.

Conclusion

Conclude the article with a summary or reflection that ties together the various elements of the story. Provide closure or leave readers with something to ponder.

- **Editing and Proofreading:** Edit and proofread your article for clarity, grammar, and style. Eliminate any errors or inconsistencies.
- **Headline and Subheadings**: Craft a headline that encapsulates the essence of the feature. Subheadings within the article can guide readers through the narrative.
- **Byline:** Include your byline at the top or bottom of the article to credit the author.
- **Ethical Considerations:** Adhere to ethical journalism principles, including accuracy, fairness, and respect for privacy.
- **Word Count:** Depending on the publication, consider word count limitations, and aim to meet them without sacrificing quality.
- **Environmental Feature:**

  "Saving Our Oceans: The Battle Against Plastic Pollution"

  This feature explores the global issue of plastic pollution in the oceans, highlighting the efforts of environmental activists, scientists, and organizations working to combat the problem.

Magazine Articles

Writing magazine articles is a versatile and creative form of journalism that caters to a wide range of readers and interests. Here are the basics of writing magazine articles:

- **Know Your Audience**: Understand your target audience's demographics, interests, and preferences. Tailor your article to appeal to their needs and expectations.
- **Choose a Compelling Topic:** Select a topic that is interesting, timely, and relevant to your audience. It should also be unique or offer a fresh perspective on a familiar subject.

- **Research Thoroughly**: Conduct in-depth research to gather facts, statistics, expert opinions, and real-life stories that will enrich your article.
- **Pitch a Unique Angle:** Find a unique angle or perspective that differentiates your article from what's already available on the topic.
- **Craft a Strong Headline:** Write a headline that is attention-grabbing and encapsulates the main point of your article. It should pique the reader's curiosity.
- **Lead with Impact**: Start with a compelling lead that draws the reader in. This could be an anecdote, a provocative question, or a surprising fact.
- **Structure and Organization**: Organize your article into sections or subheadings to make it scannable and easy to navigate. This is particularly important for long articles.
- **Engaging Writing Style**: Develop a writing style that matches the magazine's tone and audience. Use descriptive language, storytelling, and vivid imagery to engage readers.
- **Quotes and Anecdotes**: Include relevant quotes from experts, interviews, or real people who can offer insights or personal experiences related to your topic.
- **Descriptive Details:** Use descriptive details to create a vivid picture for readers. Engage the senses and make the subject come to life.
- **Supporting Evidence**: Back your claims with credible sources, statistics, and research findings to provide depth and credibility to your article.
- **Relatability:** Make the topic relatable to readers by incorporating personal experiences, emotions, and relatable situations.
- **Edit and proofread**: Thoroughly edit and proofread your article to eliminate errors, improve clarity, and refine your writing.

- **Balance Information and Entertainment**: While providing valuable information, ensure that the article is entertaining and enjoyable to read.
- **Story Arc or Narrative Flow**: Consider the narrative flow of your article. It should have a beginning, middle, and end, like a well-crafted story.
- **Call to Action or Takeaway**: Conclude with a clear call to action or a key takeaway for the reader. What should the reader do next, or what should they remember?
- **Respect Word Count**: Keep the article within the word count guidelines set by the magazine. Overly long or short articles may not fit the publication's format.
- **Photographs and Visuals**: If appropriate, suggest or include high-quality images or visual elements that complement the text.
- **Byline**: Include your byline (name of the author) to credit the writer.
- **Ethical Considerations:** Adhere to ethical journalism principles, including accuracy, fairness, and respect for privacy.

Magazine articles allow for creativity and storytelling, making them an excellent medium for reaching a broad readership. By following these basics, you can write engaging and informative magazine articles that resonate with your audience.

Farm Bulletin

Farm bulletins, also known as agricultural bulletins or extension publications, are informative documents created by agricultural extension services or organizations to provide farmers with valuable information and guidance. These bulletins serve as a means of disseminating agricultural knowledge and best practices to support sustainable farming. Here are the basics of creating effective farm bulletins:

- **Clear and Concise Language:** Use plain and straightforward language that is easily understandable by the target audience, which may include farmers with varying levels of education.
- **Targeted Information:** Focus on providing information that is relevant and beneficial to local farmers and their specific needs. Tailor the content to the region's climate, soil, crops, and livestock.

- **Use of Visuals:** Incorporate visuals such as images, diagrams, charts, and maps to enhance understanding and make the content more engaging.
- **Local Examples and Case Studies:** Include local success stories or case studies to illustrate how the information or practices have worked in the area.
- **Step-by-Step Instructions:** Provide practical, step-by-step instructions for implementing recommended practices, whether related to crop cultivation, livestock management, or pest control.
- **Highlight Benefits:** Explain the benefits of adopting the recommended practices, such as increased yield, cost savings, and sustainability.
- **Citations and References:** If applicable, provide citations and references to credible sources for further reading and verification of the information.
- **Regular Updates:** Keep the information up-to-date and reflect the latest research, technology, and best practices. Include revision dates on bulletins.
- **Distribution Channels:** Ensure effective distribution to reach the target audience. This may involve distributing printed bulletins through agricultural extension officers, local agricultural organizations, or making digital versions available online.
- **Title and Headings:** Use clear, descriptive titles and headings to help readers quickly identify the topic and content of each section.
- **Engage the Reader:** Start with an engaging introduction or story that draws readers in and communicates the importance of the information.
- **Bulleted and Numbered Lists:** Use lists to break down information into easily digestible chunks, making it more reader- friendly.
- **Call to Action:** Include a call to action or a message encouraging farmers to apply the information and seek assistance from local agricultural extension services when needed.
- **Sustainability and Environmental Considerations:** Emphasize sustainable and environmentally friendly farming practices, as they are becoming increasingly important in modern agriculture.
- **User Feedback**: Encourage feedback from farmers to continually improve the quality and relevance of the bulletins.

- **Language Options:** In areas with diverse linguistic communities, consider producing bulletins in multiple languages to reach a broader audience.
- **Local Illustrations:** Use illustrations, photos, and examples that resonate with the local culture and practices to make the content relatable.

Farm bulletins are valuable tools for disseminating agricultural knowledge, supporting farmers, and improving agricultural practices. By following these basics, you can create informative and effective bulletins that meet the needs of your target audience and contribute to sustainable agriculture.

Script Development: Crafting Compelling Narratives for Various Media

Script development is the process of crafting a script for various media, including film, television, theatre, radio, and even online content like web series and podcasts. The development process involves several stages, from an initial concept to a finalized script ready for production. Here are the key steps and considerations in script development:

- **Idea Generation:** Start by generating a compelling idea or concept for your script. This could be inspired by personal experiences, existing stories, news, or a unique creative concept.
- **Research:** Conduct research to gather information relevant to your script. This may include historical research, interviews, location scouting, or studying similar works.
- **Outline or Treatment:** Create an outline or treatment of the script. This is a summary of the story, including major plot points, character arcs, and the overall structure. It serves as a roadmap for your script.
- **Character Development:** Develop well-rounded, multi-dimensional characters. Create character profiles that include details like background, motivations, conflicts, and character arcs.
- **Script Format:** Familiarize yourself with the appropriate script format for your chosen medium (e.g., screenplay format for film and TV, stage play format for theatre).
- **Structure:** Plan the structure of your script. In a three-act structure, consider the setup, confrontation, and resolution. Ensure a clear beginning, middle, and end.

- **Dialogue:** Write authentic and engaging dialogue that suits the characters and advances the plot. Dialogue should be concise and meaningful.
- **Visual Elements:** For visual media (film, TV), consider the visual elements that enhance storytelling, including camera angles, shots, and scene descriptions.
- **Conflict and Resolution:** Develop the central conflicts and resolutions within the story. This is often the core of the narrative and keeps the audience engaged.
- **Pacing:** Balance the pacing of your script. Determine when to build tension and when to allow for moments of relief or character development.
- **Editing and Rewriting:** Expect to go through multiple drafts and revisions. Seek feedback from peers, mentors, or industry professionals, and be open to making changes.
- **Feedback:** Solicit feedback from others. It's essential to get fresh perspectives on your script to identify areas that may need improvement.
- **Budget and Practical Considerations:** Consider the budget and practical constraints when writing your script. Understand the limitations of production resources.
- **Genre and Audience:** Identify the genre of your script (e.g., drama, comedy, thriller) and define your target audience. Tailor your script to cater to the interests of that audience.
- **Legal and Copyright:** Understand copyright and legal aspects related to your script. Ensure you have the rights to use any existing material or that your original work is protected.
- **Pitching and Promotion:** If you intend to sell or produce your script, prepare a pitch or proposal. Create a logline, synopsis, and marketing materials to attract potential producers or investors.
- **Collaboration:** Recognize that scriptwriting often involves collaboration with directors, producers, actors, and other creative professionals. Be open to feedback and collaboration throughout the production process.

Script development is a creative and iterative process. Whether you're writing a screenplay, stage play, or script for other media, these steps will guide you in crafting a compelling and engaging narrative. Remember that persistence and continuous refinement are keys to successful script development.

5.2 Comprehension and Readability Testing Procedures

Comprehension and readability testing procedures are essential for ensuring that written content is understandable and effective in conveying information to the intended audience. These procedures help identify potential issues with readability and assess how well readers comprehend the material. Below are steps for conducting comprehension and readability testing:

Readability Testing

1. Choose a Readability formula

- Select a readability formula that is appropriate for your audience and content. Common options include Flesch-Kincaid Grade Level, Flesch Reading Ease, Gunning Fog Index, Coleman-Liau Index, and Automated Readability Index (ARI).

2. Apply the Readability Formula

- For printed materials, apply the formula to a representative sample of your content. For digital content, various readability tools and software are available that can analyze entire documents.

3. Interpret the Results

- Understand the readability score provided by the formula. A lower grade level or a higher reading ease score indicates easier readability. Consider whether the results match the needs of your target audience.

4. Revise the Content

- Based on the results, revise your content as needed to achieve the desired readability level. This may involve simplifying sentence structure, word choice, and overall content organization.

Comprehension Testing

1. Create Comprehension Questions

- Develop comprehension questions that cover the key points and objectives of your content. These questions should assess readers' understanding of the material.

2. Recruit Test Participants

- Identify and recruit participants who represent your target audience. Ensure that they have not been exposed to the content before testing.

3. Administer the Test

- Provide the test participants with the content you want to assess. Ask them to read the material and answer the comprehension questions.

4. Assess Responses

- Carefully evaluate the participants' responses to the comprehension questions.

  Analyze how well they understood the material and whether they answered the questions correctly.

5. Collect Feedback

- After completing the comprehension test, gather feedback from participants.

  Ask for their thoughts on the content, including any confusing or challenging aspects.

6. Revise Content as Necessary

- Use the feedback and comprehension test results to identify areas where the content needs improvement. Make revisions to address any comprehension issues.

Best Practices for both Testing Procedures

- **Target Audience**: Always consider the characteristics and literacy level of your target audience. Ensure that your content matches their needs.
- **Plain Language**: Use clear, simple language and avoid jargon or technical terms, unless your audience is well-versed in them.
- **Engaging Content**: Structure your content logically, use headings, bullet points, and visuals to enhance comprehension and engagement.
- **Iterative Process**: Both readability and comprehension testing should be part of an iterative process. Continue to test and revise your content until it effectively communicates your message to your audience.
- **Realistic Testing**: Ensure that your comprehension testing scenarios and questions realistically represent the challenges your audience may face when interacting with your content.

By following these procedures, you can improve the readability and comprehension of your content, making it more accessible and effective for your audience.

• Flesch-Kincaid Grade Level

The Flesch-Kincaid Grade Level formula is used to assess the readability of text by assigning it a grade level. The grade level indicates the education level a person needs to have to easily understand the text. Here's an example of how the formula works:

Let's take a sentence as an example: "Mary had a little lamb."

Now, we'll break down the steps to calculate the Flesch-Kincaid Grade Level for this sentence:

1. **Count the Words:** -First, count the number of words in the sentence. In our example, there are 5 words.
2. **Count the Syllables:** -Next, count the number of syllables in the sentence. To count syllables, you can either do it manually or use a tool. In this case, the sentence has 7 syllables.
3. **Calculate Average Sentence Length:** -To do this, you divide the number of words by the number of sentences in your text. Since we're just using one sentence in our example, the sentence length is 5 words.
4. **Calculate Average Syllables per word:** - Divide the number of syllables by the number of words. In our example, the average number of syllables per word is 7/5, which is 1.4.
5. **Apply the Formula**: The Flesch-Kincaid Grade Level formula is as follows:

   0.39 x Avg. Sentence length +11.80 x Avg Syllables per word – 15.59

   Plug in the values from current examples

   0.39 x 5 + 11.8 x 1.4 - 15.59
6. **Calculate the Grade Level:** - Now, calculate the final result

   1.95 + 16.52 - 15.59 = 2.88

The Flesch-Kincaid Grade Level for the sentence "Mary had a little lamb" is approximately 2.88. This means that the sentence can be easily understood by someone at a grade level of around 3. In other words, it's very simple and should be comprehensible to most readers.

Keep in mind that this is just a single-sentence example. When working with longer texts, you would calculate the average values across the entire text to determine the overall readability

5.3 Story Board Preparation

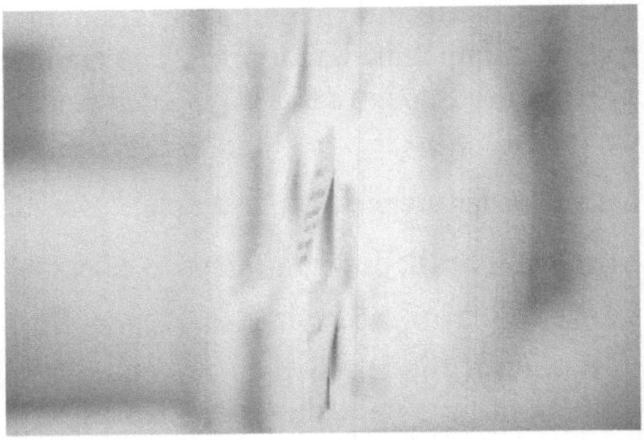

Storyboarding is a crucial step in the pre- production process for various visual storytelling mediums, including film, animation, commercial, and multimedia presentations. A storyboard is a visual representation of the narrative, where each frame or panel illustrates a scene or shot. Here's a guide on how to prepare a storyboard:

- **Understand Your Story:** Familiarize yourself with the script or narrative that you'll be storyboarding. Understand the characters, locations, and key events in the story.
- **Gather Your Materials:** You'll need materials such as paper, a storyboard template, or digital tools like storyboard software or apps. Choose what works best for your project.
- **Divide Your Story:** Break down your narrative into scenes or sequences. Identify the main story beats and the transitions between them.
- **Create Thumbnails:** In each panel of your storyboard, create rough thumbnail sketches that represent the composition of the shot. These sketches should be simple and quick, focusing on the key elements and characters.
- **Add Details:** Include essential details in each panel, such as camera angles, character positions, expressions, and any significant props or objects.
- **Write Descriptions:** Below or next to each panel, write brief descriptions of what's happening in the scene. This can include dialogue, action descriptions, or notes to provide context.
- **Number your Panels:** Number your panels or frames sequentially to ensure the correct order of shots and scenes.
- **Pay Attention to Shot Composition**: Consider the visual composition of each shot.

Think about framing, camera angles, and any specific visual motifs or symbols that are relevant to the story.

- **Be Consistent:** Maintain consistency in terms of character placement, size, and proportion throughout the storyboard. This ensures that the visuals accurately reflect the story.
- **Visualize Movement:** If your project involves action or movement, use directional arrows or motion lines to indicate the direction and speed of movement.
- **Seek Feedback:** Share your storyboard with others, such as the director, producer, or colleagues, to gather feedback and make necessary revisions.
- **Revise and Refine:** Based on feedback, make revisions to your storyboard. Ensure that it accurately reflects the vision of the project.
- **Include Notes and Annotations:** Use callout boxes or notes to include additional details, technical instructions, or references for props, costumes, or set design.
- **Color or Style Choices:** Depending on your project, you may choose to add color, shading, or a particular stylistic approach to your storyboard panels.
- **Finalize Your Storyboard:** - Once you're satisfied with your storyboard and have incorporated feedback, finalize it for presentation and use during production.
- **Presentation Format:** Decide on the format for presenting your storyboard. This could be in a digital document, printed sheets, or via a storyboard software application.
- **Use Storyboard for Guidance:** During the production phase, refer to your storyboard as a visual guide to ensure that the scenes are shot or animated as intended.

Storyboarding is an essential step in the filmmaking and visual storytelling process, helping to visualize and plan the execution of a project. It aids in communication, collaboration, and ensuring that the final product aligns with the director's or creator's vision.

5.4 Profile Writing

Profile writing and feature writing are both forms of non-fiction writing used in journalism and other publications. While they often overlap, they do have distinct characteristics and purposes.

Definition: A profile piece focuses on a particular individual (or sometimes a group or place) and seeks to provide a deeper understanding of the subject by exploring their background, characteristics, experiences, and impact.

Purpose: To provide insight into the life, character, and significance of the subject. Profiles often humanize their subjects and make them relatable to the reader.

Content

- **Background**: information about the subject's upbringing, education, and early experiences.
- **Character:** Personal attributes, habits, passions, and quirks.
- **Achievements:** Significant accomplishments and their impact
- **Challenges:** Obstacles faced and how they were overcome.
- **Interviews** are essential in profile writing. Direct conversations with the subject provide firsthand insights, while interviews with friends, family, or colleagues can give additional perspectives.
- **Narrative Structure:** Profiles often use a narrative structure to recount events in the subject's life. Anecdotes and stories can bring the profile to life.

5.5 Magazine Journalism

Magazine journalism refers to the practice of producing and writing content for magazines. Magazine journalism covers a wide range of topics and styles, and it involves in-depth research, reporting, and writing to engage and inform readers. Here are key aspects of magazine journalism:

- **Magazine Genres:** Magazines cover a diverse array of genres, including lifestyle, fashion, travel, entertainment, health, science, technology, politics, and more. Each genre has its own unique style and target audience.
- **Features and Long-Form Journalism**: Many magazines feature long-form articles that delve deep into a subject, issue, or profile. These articles

often combine research, interviews, and storytelling to provide an in-depth exploration of the topic.

- **Profiles and Interviews**: Magazines frequently publish profiles of individuals, including celebrities, entrepreneurs, artists, and everyday people with remarkable stories. Interviews are a common feature in magazine journalism.
- **Investigative Journalism**: Some magazines are known for their investigative journalism, which involves in-depth research, fact-checking, and uncovering hidden information on important topics.
- **Opinion and Commentary**: Magazines often provide a platform for writers and experts to express their opinions and viewpoints. This can take the form of columns, essays, and editorial content.
- **Visual Elements**: Magazine journalism incorporates visual elements such as photographs, illustrations, infographics, and captions. Visuals enhance the storytelling and can be as important as the text.
- **Audience and Niche**: Magazines cater to specific audiences and niches. Understanding the target readership is crucial in magazine journalism, as it influences the tone, content, and style of articles.
- **Freelance and Staff Writers**: Many magazine writers are freelancers who contribute articles to various publications. Some writers are full-time staff members of specific magazines.
- **Editing and Fact-Checking:** Magazines have editors and fact-checkers to ensure the accuracy and quality of content. Editors work with writers to refine articles, while fact- checkers verify the information.
- **Ethics and Style:** Magazine journalism adheres to journalistic ethics, including fairness, accuracy, and objectivity. Magazines may also have a unique style guide and voice that sets them apart.
- **Print and Digital Formats:** While traditional print magazines remain popular, many magazines also have a digital presence through websites and digital editions. Writers should adapt their content to the chosen format.

- **Pitching and Submission**: Freelance writers often pitch their article ideas to magazine editors. They must tailor their pitches to the magazine's style and audience.
- **Layout and Design**: Magazines pay careful attention to layout and design. The way articles are visually presented on the page or screen can impact the reader's experience.
- **Publication Schedule:** Magazines are typically published on a regular schedule, such as monthly, bimonthly, or quarterly. Writers must adhere to deadlines.
- **Engaging Headlines and Subheads:** Magazine articles use engaging headlines and subheadings to draw readers into the content.

Magazine journalism offers a diverse and creative platform for writers and journalists to explore various subjects, tell compelling stories, and contribute to the broader media landscape. It allows for in-depth reporting and storytelling that can inform, entertain, and inspire readers.

5.6 Feature Writing

Definition: A feature story delves deep into a particular topic, idea, event, or trend. While it might include profiles of people related to the topic, it isn't centred on one individual.

Purpose: To provide a detailed and comprehensive look at a particular subject. Features are often longer and more in-depth than regular news stories.

Content

- **Background:** Setting the scene and providing context for the feature's main topic.
- **Detail:** Extensive information and different viewpoints on the subject.
- **Human Element:** Real-life stories or interviews that connect the larger topic to personal experiences.
- **Research:** Feature stories require thorough research. This includes interviews, but also document reviews, observations, and other data sources.
- **Structure**: Features can be more flexible in structure than news articles. Writers might employ a variety of narrative techniques, like scene-setting, flashbacks, or parallel storylines.

Similarities

- **In-depth Approach:** Both profiles and features provide a deep dive into their subjects.
- **Human Interest:** Both aim to connect with readers on a human level making stories and subjects relatable.
- **Use of Description:** Rich, descriptive language is often employed to paint a vivid picture for the reader.

Differences

- **Focus:** Profiles zero in on an individual or group, while features tackle broader topics or themes.
- **Scope:** Features often have a broader scope, pulling in various elements to illuminate a topic, whereas profiles stay anchored to their main subject.
- **Sources:** While both rely on interviews, features often require more diverse sources to capture the breadth of the topic.

In both forms of writing, it's essential to maintain accuracy, fairness, and a balanced perspective, as these articles often provide readers with a deeper understanding of their subjects than shorter news stories.

5.7 Radio Journalism

Radio journalism is a form of journalism that focuses on creating news and content for radio broadcasts. It plays a crucial role in informing, entertaining, and engaging audiences through audio storytelling. Here are the key aspects of radio journalism:

1. **Audio Reporting:** Radio journalism primarily relies on the medium of sound. Journalists use audio recordings, interviews, natural sound, and narration to create stories for radio broadcasts.
2. **News Reports:** Radio journalists produce news reports that are typically shorter and more concise than print or online articles. These reports often include headlines, lead stories, and brief summaries of events.
3. **Feature Stories:** In addition to news reports, radio journalism also includes feature stories that delve deeper into various topics, providing in-depth coverage and analysis.

4. **Live Broadcasts:** Many radio stations offer live news broadcasts, where journalists report on breaking news, events, and developments as they happen. These live reports can include interviews, eyewitness accounts, and updates.

5. **Scripted Narration:** Radio journalists write scripts for news reports and feature stories. These scripts are designed to be read aloud and should be clear, concise, and engaging. Journalists often record their own voiceovers or work with voice talent.

6. **Interviews:** Interviews are a fundamental part of radio journalism. Journalists interview experts, witnesses, and newsmakers to gather information and insights for their stories. Interviews are typically edited and integrated into news reports.

7. **Sound Editing:** Radio journalists use sound editing software to mix and edit audio clips. This can involve adding music, sound effects, and adjusting audio levels to create a polished and engaging final product.

8. **Storytelling:** Effective storytelling is essential in radio journalism. Journalists use narrative techniques, descriptive language, and pacing to engage listeners and convey the significance of the news or feature.

9. **Production Values:** Radio journalism places a strong emphasis on production values. High-quality sound recording and editing, as well as clear and expressive narration, contribute to the overall impact of the story.

10. **Audience Engagement:** Radio journalists consider their target audience and tailor their content to the preferences and interests of listeners. They aim to captivate and inform their audience effectively.

11. **Adaptation for Digital Media: Ia**nthe digital age, radio journalism often extends to digital platforms, where audio content is available as podcasts or on websites. Radio journalists may also integrate social media and multimedia elements into their work.

12. **Ethics and Accuracy:** Radio journalists, like their print and digital counterparts, are committed to journalistic ethics, including accuracy, fairness, and objectivity in reporting.

13. Co**llaboration:** Radio journalism often involves collaboration with sound engineers, producers, and other professionals to create high-quality broadcasts.

Radio journalism has evolved alongside technological advancements, offering new opportunities for creative storytelling. It remains a vital source of news and information for a wide range of audiences, with a unique ability to reach and engage people through the power of sound.

Principles and practices for gathering, writing, and producing news for radio

Principles and practices for gathering, writing, and producing news for radio are essential for ensuring the quality and effectiveness of radio journalism. These principles guide radio journalists in delivering accurate, timely, and engaging news content to their audiences. Here are the key principles and practices in radio journalism:

Principles

- **Accuracy**: Accuracy is paramount in radio journalism. Reporters must verify facts, double-check information, and cross-reference sources to ensure that the news is reliable and truthful.
- **Objectivity**: Journalists should maintain objectivity and impartiality in their reporting. They must present different perspectives and let the audience form their own opinions.
- **Timeliness:** Radio news is often expected to be the first source of breaking news. Therefore, journalists must work quickly to report events as they unfold and provide real-time updates.
- **Relevance:** Stories should be selected and prioritized based on their relevance to the audience. What matters most to the community or target audience should be at the forefront.
- **Clarity:** Radio news should be clear and concise. Complex information should be presented in an easy-to-understand manner. Use straightforward language and avoid jargon.
- **Local Focus**: Local news has particular significance on the radio. Priorities stories that directly affect the community you serve.
- **Fairness:** Ensure that all parties involved in a story have the opportunity to comment and provide their perspective. Balance and fairness are critical in journalism.
- **Ethical Conduct**: Adhere to ethical guidelines and codes of conduct for journalism. Respect the privacy and dignity of individuals mentioned in news stories.

- **Audio Quality:** Pay attention to audio quality. The sound should be clear, and audio clips should be free from background noise or distortion.
- **Engagement:** Engage the audience by using storytelling techniques, audio clips, and sound effects to make news stories more compelling.

Practices

- **Research:** Gather information through research, interviews, and official sources. Verify the facts and confirm the credibility of your sources.
- **Writing for the Ear:** Radio news is meant to be heard, not read. Write in a way that is conversational, engaging, and easily comprehensible when spoken.
- **Scripting**: Create scripts that include lead-ins, segues, and natural pauses to facilitate smooth transitions between news stories.
- **Interviewing:** Conduct interviews with skill and professionalism. Prepare questions in advance, actively listen, and ask follow-up questions to gather comprehensive information.
- **Editing:** Edit audio clips and narration carefully to remove unnecessary elements and maintain the story's flow. Ensure that sound bites are relevant and concise.
- **Voice and Delivery:** Work on your voice modulation, pace, and clarity. Your delivery should be engaging and authoritative while remaining conversational.
- **Newscast Structure:** Organize your newscast with a clear structure. Typically, it begins with the most important story (the "lead"), followed by other news items in descending order of importance.
- **Soundscape**: Incorporate natural sound, music, and sound effects when appropriate to create a vivid listening experience.
- **Collaboration:** Collaborate with producers, editors, and fellow journalists to ensure a cohesive and well-coordinated news production process.
- **Audience Feedback**: Be open to feedback from your audience and colleagues. Use feedback to refine your skills and improve your reporting. These principles and practices are vital for radio journalists to deliver news that is informative, engaging, and trustworthy. Effective radio journalism plays a significant role in keeping the public informed and upholding democratic values.

5.8 Television Journalism

Gathering, writing, and producing news for television requires adherence to specific principles and practices to ensure that the news is presented accurately, ethically, and effectively. Here are the key principles and practices:

1. Accuracy and Verification

Principle: The foremost principle of television news is accuracy. Information must be fact- checked and verified before it is broadcast.

Practice: Journalists should rely on multiple credible sources to verify facts. Avoid reporting unverified information or rumours:

2. Objectivity and Fairness

Principle: Television news should be presented in an objective and fair manner, without bias or personal opinion.

Practice: Reporters and anchors should present information in a balanced and impartial way, providing a platform for diverse perspectives.

3. Timeliness

Principle: Television news is focused on providing the most up-to-date information to the audience.

Practice: News stories are produced and broadcast promptly to keep viewers informed about current events. Breaking news should be covered as it happens.

4. Clarity and Simplicity

Principle: News should be presented in a clear and easily understandable manner.

Practice: Journalists use straightforward language, avoid jargon, and use visuals to make complex stories accessible to a broad audience.

5. Visual Storytelling

Principle: Television is a visual medium, and storytelling should utilize visuals to enhance the narrative.

Practice: Use images, video footage, graphics, and maps to illustrate and support the story. Visuals should complement the content and add context.

6. Ethical Reporting

Principle: Ethical standards, such as respecting privacy and minimizing harm, are integral to responsible journalism.

Practice: Journalists should obtain consent for interviews and respect the privacy of individuals, especially in sensitive situations. Minimize harm by not endangering sources or revealing sensitive information.

7. Editorial Independence

Principle: Journalists and news organizations should maintain editorial independence from external influences.

Practice: Avoid conflicts of interest, political pressure, or commercial interests that could compromise the integrity of news reporting.

8. Transparency

Principle: Honesty and transparency with the audience are essential for building trust.

Practice: Acknowledge and correct errors promptly. Disclose any relationships or affiliations that could be perceived as a conflict of interest.

9. Story Selection

Principles: The editorial team should select news stories based on their importance and relevance to the audience.

Practice: Prioritize stories that have a significant impact on the community and are of general interest. Avoid sensationalism or focusing excessively on celebrity or trivial news.

10. Diversity and Inclusivity

Principle: Reflect the diversity of society in news coverage and newsroom staff.

Practice: Ensure that the newsroom is diverse, and cover stories that represent the experiences and perspectives of different communities.

11. Story Development and Structure

Principle: Effective storytelling is crucial in television news.

Practice: Develop news stories with a clear structure, including an attention-grabbing lead, context, main points, and a conclusion. Use compelling visuals to support the narrative.

12. Production Quality

Principle: High production values are important for the credibility and engagement of television news.

Practice: Pay attention to technical quality, including camera work, lighting, audio, and graphics. Ensure that the production enhances the storytelling.

13. Audience Engagement

Principle: Engaging the audience is essential for the success of television news.

Practice: Use interactive elements, such as live audience polls, social media integration, and user-generated content, to involve the audience in the news process.

These principles and practices guide television journalists and producers in creating news content that informs, educates, and engages the audience while upholding ethical and journalistic standards. The effective use of visuals and the ability to tell compelling stories are central to the success of television news reporting.

5.9 Photo journalism - Visual Language, Skills And Techniques

Photo journalism refers to the use of photography to tell news stories. Photo journalism relies on the visual language of photography to communicate news stories, events, and issues. It combines elements of art and journalism to convey the facts, emotions, and impact of a situation. Photo journalism use specific skills and techniques to capture compelling and informative images. Here are some key aspects of the visual language, skills, and techniques in photo journalism:

Visual Language

1. **Composition**: To produce balanced and aesthetically pleasing shots, photojournalists use compositional principles including the rule of thirds and leading lines. The viewer's attention is drawn to the main subject and story via a thoughtful composition.
2. **Framing**: Framing is bringing attention to the subject of the picture by utilizing components such as windows or doorways. This method gives the picture more depth and meaning.
3. **Point of View**: The viewer's perception can be greatly influenced by the choice of camera angle and perspective. Whether taking shots from an uncommon angle or at eye level, photojournalists always select perspectives that best tell the narrative.
4. **Lighting**: It's important to comprehend and work with light. Natural light can set in a variety of ways, including the gentle glow of dawn or the intense contrast of midday sunlight.
5. **Story telling:** Photography acts as a tool for narrative. Photographers may tell stories and arouse feelings by encapsulating experiences, feelings, and context in a single frame.
6. **Colour and Tone**: A photograph's mood and ambiance are influenced by the colour selection, colour harmony, and post-processing modifications.
7. **Negative Space:** Negative space (areas without significant detail) can be used to create contrast and draw attention to the subject.

Skills and Techniques

1. **Story telling**: A skilled photo journalism can convey the entire narrative within a single frame. The ability to capture the decisive moment, where action and emotion align, is essential.
2. **Timing**: Timing is critical in photo journalism. Being in the right place at the right time to capture a significant moment can make all the difference in the impact of an image.
3. **Quick Decision-Making:** Photo journalism often have to make fast decisions about composition, exposure settings, and focal length while in the field.
4. **Interaction and Access:** Building trust and rapport with subjects allows photo journalism to capture authentic moments. Access to restricted or sensitive areas often depends on trust and negotiation.

5. **Technical Proficiency:** Understanding camera settings, equipment, and post- processing techniques is a basic requirement. Proficiency in these technical aspects ensures that the image is properly exposed and edited.
6. **Captioning and Context:** Providing detailed captions or context for the image is a key practice in photo journalism. Captions offer the viewer essential information to understand the story.
7. **Ethical Considerations:** Photo journalism must navigate ethical dilemmas and ensure their work adheres to professional standards. This includes issues like informed consent, privacy, and image manipulation.
8. **Adaptability:** Photo journalism need to adapt to various situations and environments, whether they are covering a natural disaster, a sports event, or a political rally.

5.10 Photography, Principles and use in Extension

Photography is a powerful medium with a wide range of principles and applications, including its use in extension programs. Extension programs often associated with agriculture, community development, education, and more, can benefit from photography in various ways. Here, we'll explore the principles of photography and its use in extension work:

Photography Principles

Knowing the properties of light, like direction, intensity, and colour temperature is essential. Shadows may be removed, subjects can be highlighted, and moods can be created.

- **Exposure:** Proper exposure, achieved through control of aperture shutter speed, and ISO settings, ensures that an image is neither too dark nor too bright. Exposure impacts the clarity and quality of the photograph.
- **Story telling:** Photography acts as a tool for narrative. Photographers may tell stories and arouse feelings by encapsulating experiences feelings, and context in a single frame.
- **Colour and Tone**: A photograph's mood and ambiance are influenced by colour selection, color harmony, and post-processing modifications.
- **Composition:** To direct the viewer's eye and convey the appropriate message, one needs carefully consider how things are arranged within a frame.

Use of Photography in Extension

- **Documentation:** Photography can be used to document agricultural practices, community events, and development projects. These visual records are valuable for assessment, monitoring progress, and illustrating success stories.
- **Education and Training:** Photographs can be incorporated into training materials and presentations to enhance the learning experience. Visual aids can simplify complex concepts and demonstrate proper techniques.
- **Communication:** Images are universal and can bridge language barriers. They can be used in brochures, newsletters, websites, and social media to convey messages and engage the target audience.
- **Advocacy and Fundraising**: Powerful images can be a compelling tool for advocacy campaigns and fundraising efforts. They can show the impact of programs and the needs of communities.
- **Community Engagement:** Involving community members in photography projects can be empowering and foster a sense of ownership. Photo exhibits or storytelling through photographs can engage the community.
- **Monitoring and Evaluation:** Photographs serve as visual data for monitoring and evaluating the impact of extension programs. They provide concrete evidence of changes and progress.
- **Reportage and Story telling**: Extension professionals can use photojournalism to tell stories of the people and places they work with. Photo essays and narratives can create a connection with the audience.
- **Crisis and Disaster Management:** During crises or natural disasters, photography can document damage, response efforts, and recovery, aiding in planning and coordination.

Photography, when used effectively, can enhance extension programs, create awareness, and drive positive change. It's a versatile tool for capturing moments, conveying messages, and connecting with the audience, making it an invaluable asset for extension professionals.

5.11 New Media Journalsim -Websites, Blogs, and Social Media

New media journalism encompasses various digital platforms, including websites, blogs, and social media, to report, share news, and engage with audiences. This form of journalism has expanded the way news is produced and consumed, making information more accessible and interactive. Here's an overview of new media journalism on websites, blogs, and social media:

1. News Websites

Traditional media outlets often have online versions of their newspapers or TV stations. These websites provide timely news updates, in-depth articles, and multimedia content.

- **Independent News Websites:** A plethora of independent news websites have surfaced, providing investigative journalism and different points of view on a range of subjects.
- **Multimedia Integration:** To improve storytelling and engagement, news websites integrate multimedia components including videos, infographics, and interactive features.
- **Archiving and Searchability**: Websites offer an article archive, which facilitates readers' access to previous news pieces. This feature is known as "searchability." Search functions assist users in locating particular information

2. Blogs

- **Citizen Journalism:** Blogs facilitate the dissemination of news, viewpoints, and firsthand accounts by citizen journalists. They offer a variety of topics and frequently present opposing views.
- **Niche Reporting**: Writers frequently concentrate on particular niches, such as politics, technology, travel, or lifestyle, and offer comprehensive reporting in these domains.
- **Commentary and Analysis:** Opinion leaders and contributors to public conversation, a large number of bloggers provide commentary and analysis on current affairs.

- **Interactivity:** Blogs foster discussion and a sense of community by allowing readers to engage directly through comments.

3. Social Networking

- **Real-time Updates:** Real-time updates on breaking news and events are provided via social media platforms such as Twitter. They come in especially handy in times of need and crisis.
- **User-Generated Content**: People can report news, and contribute videos, photographs, and personal experiences, and social media platforms encourage this type of content.
- **Communication with Audience:** Journalists and media organizations utilize social media platforms to communicate with their readers, disseminate stories, obtain opinions, and carry out surveys or polls.
- **Visual Story telling:** News content is presented visually on platforms such as Instagram and TikTok through brief films and photographs.
- **Fact-Checking and Verification:** Social media can additionally be used to refute misleading information and verify information. Many organizations and individuals strive to verify and rectify false information in the news.
- **Live broadcasting:** Using sites like Facebook and YouTube for live broadcasting

Challenges and Considerations

- **Accuracy and Verification:** Information on social media can be unverified and spread rapidly. Journalists need to be vigilant about verifying sources and information.
- **Ethical Issues:** Journalists must navigate ethical issues related to privacy, sourcing, and conflicts of interest, especially when engaging on social media.
- **Monetization:** Many independent bloggers and new media websites struggle with monetization and sustainability.
- **Filter Bubbles:** Algorithms on social media platforms can create filter bubbles, where users are exposed only to content that aligns with their existing beliefs.
- **Online Harassment:** Journalists and bloggers may face online harassment and threats, particularly when reporting on sensitive or controversial topics.

New media journalism offers a wealth of opportunities to reach broader audiences and engage with readers in novel ways. However, it also presents challenges related to accuracy, ethics, and the evolving media landscape. Journalists and media organizations must adapt to these digital platforms to effectively report, share news, and foster informed discussions.

5.12 Responsible Journalism, Fairness and Balance

Responsible journalism, fairness, and balance are essential principles that guide ethical and credible journalism. These principles ensure that news reporting is accurate, unbiased, and serves the public interest. Here's a closer look at each of these concepts:

Responsible Journalism

Responsible journalism refers to the practice of journalism with a strong commitment to ethical standards, accountability, and professionalism. It involves the following key aspects:

- **Truth and Accuracy:** Responsible journalism prioritizes truth and accuracy. Journalists should strive to report facts, verify information, and correct errors promptly.
- **Independence:** Journalists should maintain their independence from political, commercial, and other interests that could compromise their objectivity and integrity.
- **Accountability:** Journalists and media organizations should be accountable for their work. They should be willing to address public concerns and criticisms and provide recourse for grievances.
- **Minimizing Harm:** Responsible journalism aims to minimize harm to individuals, communities, and society as a whole. This includes exercising sensitivity when reporting on sensitive or traumatic topics.
- **Transparency:** Journalists should be transparent about their sources, methods, and conflicts of interest. Transparency helps build trust with the audience.

Fairness

Fairness in journalism is the principle of treating all individuals, groups, or perspectives equitably, without favouritism or bias. It includes the following components:

- **Balanced Reporting:** Fairness involves providing balanced coverage that represents different viewpoints, ensuring that all sides of a story are heard and given due consideration.
- **Impartiality:** Journalists should approach their work with impartiality, setting aside personal biases and opinions to report objectively.
- **Right of Reply:** Fair journalism often provides the right of reply to individuals or organizations mentioned in a story. This allows them to respond to allegations or criticisms.
- **Avoiding Stereotypes and Discrimination:** Journalists should avoid reinforcing stereotypes or engaging in discriminatory practices in their reporting.

Balance

Balance is a key element of fair journalism and refers to providing proportionate and equal coverage to different sides or aspects of a story. This principle entails:

- **Inclusion of Diverse Perspectives**: Balanced reporting includes a variety of voices, perspectives, and opinions. It ensures that minority views or underrepresented groups are not marginalized.
- **Contextual Reporting:** Journalists should provide context for the events they are reporting on, helping the audience to understand the broader picture and the implications of the story.
- **Avoiding False Equivalence:** Balance does not mean giving equal time or weight to all viewpoints, especially when one side is based on false information or lacks credibility. Journalists should differentiate between legitimate perspectives and misinformation.
- **Prioritizing Accuracy:** In the pursuit of balance, journalists should never compromise on accuracy. Balance should not be achieved by including false or misleading information.

Responsible journalism, fairness, and balance are crucial for maintaining public trust in the media and for the media's role in a democratic society. Journalists and media organizations should adhere to these principles to provide credible and informative news that serves the public interest.

Libel

Libel is a type of defamation commonly used in journalism and communication. It happens when inaccurate and harmful statements—whether printed or written—are sent to a third party or published, affecting the reputation of a person, group, or other institution. Libel is a significant legal matter that can result in lawsuits and financial losses in the event that the aggrieved party can demonstrate that the remarks were untrue and caused them harm. The following are important facets of libel in the media:

Elements of Libel

- **False Statement:** A statement needs to be untrue in order to qualify as libel. A common defense against libelous accusations is the truth.
- **Publication:** The misleading statement must be made public or shared with a third party, not simply the creator or a select few.
- **Harm:** The false statement must harm the reputation of the subject. This harm could appear as reputational harm, lost revenue, psychological discomfort, or other observable and verifiable losses.
- **Identification**: The statement's subject needs to be recognizable. It could be any identifiable person, group, business, or other entity that the audience or readers can make out.
- **Fault**: The plaintiff, or the party suing for defamation, may occasionally have to provide evidence that the remark was actually said.

5.13 Commercial Nature of the Media

The term "commercial nature of the media" describes how many media outlets, such as periodicals, websites, radio stations, television stations, and newspapers, are financially driven by and depend on advertising, subscription fees, or sales revenue to remain in business. The following are some salient features of the media's commercial nature:

Revenue Sources

- **Advertising:** A significant source of revenue for media organisations is advertising.

  Businesses sponsor media channels with ads to advertise their goods and services. The cash generated from advertising can be a significant source of income, especially for online and television media.
- **Subscriptions and Sales:** Digital paywalls, newsstand sales, and subscriptions are a source of income for certain media companies, including newspapers and magazines. Consumers pay for content availability.

- **Sponsorship and Product Placement:** Apart from conventional advertising, certain media outlets could showcase sponsored content or product placement, wherein businesses compensate for integrating their goods or messaging into media material.
- **Digital Models:** Online media outlets frequently depend on a mix of digital memberships and advertising. Platforms could provide a combination of paid and free content.

1. **Profit Motive:** Media organisations frequently have a profit motive, which means that their goal is to make a profit for their owners or shareholders by generating revenue that surpasses their expenses. These companies need to be profitable in order to survive.
2. **Market Competition:** The media industry is highly competitive. Media outlets must create information that is interesting, timely, and, frequently, appealing to a certain target group so as to attract viewers and sponsors.
3. **Audience Attention:** Media organizations aim to attract in and hold the attention of their audience. Increased online engagement, viewing, or readership can result in higher advertising rates and, ultimately, increased revenue.
4. **Content Choices:** The media's commercial nature can influence choices of content. Popular material, content that appeals to advertisers, or content which meets the tastes of their target audience may be given priority by media organizations.
5. **Ethical Considerations:** Media organizations have to deal with moral dilemmas that sometimes result from their business goals. It is a never-ending task to strike a balance between the pursuit of profit and ethical standards and responsible journalism.
6. **Media Ownership:** Owners of media organizations include multinational corporations, individual investors, and big businesses. The ownership structure of a media organization can have an impact on its priorities and editorial direction.
7. **Market Dynamics:** Market variables, such as supply and demand, industry mergers, and shifts in advertising patterns, have an impact on the media landscape. For media companies to stay competitive, they must adjust to these market dynamics.

The capacity to support excellent journalism and a diverse range of media channels are just two benefits of the media's economic model, but it also raises concerns about the possibility of bias, sensationalism, and conflict of interest. For media organizations to give the public accurate, moral, and reliable information, they must strike a balance between their business interests and their journalistic obligations.

5.14 Constructive Criticism in Journalism

Constructive criticism in journalism plays a critical role in improving the quality and integrity of news reporting. Journalists, editors, and media organizations rely on feedback and critique to enhance their work. Here are some ways constructive criticism is applied in journalism:

- **Peer Review and Editorial Feedback**: Journalists often seek input and critique from colleagues, senior editors, and mentors before publishing their stories. This helps identify inaccuracies, biases, or ethical concerns and improves the overall quality of reporting.
- **Reader Feedback:** Media outlets encourage readers to provide feedback on their stories through comments, letters to the editor, or online forums. Constructive feedback from the audience can help journalists address errors, clarify points, or offer different perspectives.
- **Ombudsmen and Public Editors:** Many media organizations employ ombudsmen or public editors who serve as independent watchdogs, collecting and addressing reader complaints and concerns. They offer constructive critiques and advocate for responsible journalism within the organization.
- **Ethics Committees:** Media outlets may establish ethics committees to assess ethical issues in journalism, such as conflicts of interest, accuracy, and fairness. These committees provide guidance and recommendations to uphold journalistic standards.
- **Columbia Journalism Review and Other Media Watchdog Groups:** Independent organizations like the Columbia Journalism Review (CJR) and other media watchdog groups monitor and critique journalism practices. They provide analysis and recommendations for improvement.
- **Media Ethics Codes**: Many journalism associations and organizations, such as the Society of Professional Journalists (SPJ) and the Associated Press (AP), have codes of ethics that provide guidelines for responsible reporting. Constructive criticism often references these codes when evaluating journalistic practices.

- **Credibility and Trust Studies:** Journalists and media organizations analyze studies and surveys that assess public trust and credibility in journalism. Constructive criticism based on the findings of these studies can lead to changes in newsroom practices.
- **Internal Editorial Meetings:** Regular editorial meetings within media organizations provide opportunities for journalists and editors to discuss stories, editorial decisions, and ethical considerations. This process includes feedback and constructive critique to improve coverage.
- **Feedback from Diversity and Inclusion Initiatives**: Media organizations may implement diversity and inclusion initiatives to ensure more balanced and equitable reporting. Constructive criticism stemming from these initiatives can lead to changes in newsroom culture and representation.
- **Academic Research**: Journalism scholars and researchers often conduct studies and analysis of media content and practices. Their findings can serve as sources of constructive criticism and suggestions for journalistic improvement.
- **Social Media Feedback:** Journalists may receive feedback and critique from their audience on social media platforms. While not all comments may be constructive, insightful feedback can help improve reporting.
- **Self-Reflection and Ethical Practices:** Journalists can engage in self-reflection and adhere to ethical practices. They are encouraged to scrutinize their own work, acknowledge their biases, and seek ways to improve their reporting.

Constructive criticism is an integral part of the journalistic process, helping journalists and media organizations uphold ethical standards, maintain credibility, and provide accurate and responsible news coverage. It fosters transparency, accountability, and continuous improvement in the field of journalism.

5.15 Advertisement -Principles and Practices

A product, service, idea, or organization is promoted to a particular audience through advertising, which is a type of communication. It's a marketing tactic meant to enlighten, convince, and sway consumers to do a certain action, such as buying a product, utilizing a service, contributing to a cause, or raising awareness. In order to create ads that effectively attract the target audience's attention, deliver a message, and motivate desired behaviours, certain guidelines and best practices must be followed. Here are some essential advertising practices and concepts for print, web, and television media:

Principles

- **Know Your Audience:** Identify the needs, interests, and demographics of your target audience. Make your message relevant to them.
- **Clarity and Simplicity:** Ensure the message is comprehensible, brief, and clear. Be clear of excessive complexity and jargon
- **Unique Selling Proposition (USP):** Emphasize the features that set your product or service apart from the competition. Point out and highlight a particular advantage.
- **Emotion and Story telling:** Establish a connection with the audience by using emotional appeal and story telling. Narratives and comparable experiences tend to elicit a response from people.
- **Visual Impact:** Create visually striking advertisements by utilizing captivating pictures, colours, and design elements. Visual components may immediately grab attention and communicate ideas.
- **Consistency:** Ensure that all advertisements and platforms use the same logos, slogans, and graphic components to maintain a consistent brand identity.
- **Call to Action (CTA):** Encourage visitors to do something, such as buy something, register, or get in touch with your company. A strong call to action is essential.
- **Testing and Data:** Monitor the efficacy of your advertisements with data and analytics. Ad effectiveness can be improved with the utilisation of A/B testing and other strategies.
- **Honesty and Transparency:** When you advertise, be truthful and open. Be clear of misleading information, deceitful techniques, and false claims.

Practices

- **Market Research**: Conduct thorough market research to understand your target audience, competitors, and industry trends. Use this data to inform your advertising strategy.
- **Creative Concept**: Develop a unique and creative concept for your ad campaign. This could include a catchy slogan, a memorable visual, or a captivating storyline.
- **Media Planning**: Choose the right media channels to reach your target audience. This might include television, radio, print, digital advertising, social media, or a combination of these.
- **Content Creation:** Create compelling ad content, whether it's copy images, videos, or a combination. Ensure it aligns with your target audience and advertising goals.
- **Budget Management:** Allocate your advertising budget strategically. Determine how much you can spend on each channel and campaign to maximize the return on investment.
- **Testing your campaign:** Before launching a large-scale campaign, think about conducting smaller tests to hone your strategy and messaging.
- **Monitoring and Modifications:** Keep an eye on the effectiveness of your advertisements at all times, and be prepared to make changes as needed. This could entail reallocating the funding, altering the target audience, or changing the messaging.
- **Engagement and Interaction:** Promote participation by the public through activities like answering social media comments or implementing crowd-driven interactive marketing.
- **Legal and Ethical Compliance:** Verify that your advertisements adhere to all applicable laws and industry norms. This entails abstaining from copyright violations, abiding by privacy laws, and refraining from making deceptive statements.
- **Measurement and Evaluation**: Apply key performance indicators (KPIs) like as click- through rates, conversion rates, and return on investment to assess the effectiveness of your advertising initiatives.
- **Feedback and Iteration:** Collect feedback from your audience and stakeholders to identify areas for improvement. Use this feedback to refine future ad campaigns.

Effective advertising requires a combination of creativity, strategic planning, and a deep understanding of your target audience. By following these principles and practices, you can create advertising campaigns that have a greater impact and deliver the desired results.

5.16 Let's Evaluate

1. **What is the primary characteristic of a news story?**

   a. In-depth analysis
   b. Creative storytelling
   c. Timeliness and objectivity
   d. Fictional elements

2. **Feature articles often differ from news stories in that they**

   a. Emphasize brevity and conciseness
   b. Focus on current events and breaking news
   c. Allow for creative storytelling and exploration of human interest
   d. Prioritize objectivity and neutrality

3. **What is a common feature of magazine articles that distinguishes them from newspaper articles?**

   a. short word count and minimal details
   b. Frequent use of jargon and technical language
   c. A longer narrative style and more in-depth content
   d. Strict adherence to the inverted pyramid structure

4. **What is the purpose of a farm bulletin?**

   a. To provide a comprehensive guide to city living
   b. To offer an overview of local politics
   c. To disseminate agricultural information to farmers
   d. To promote cultural events and entertainment

5. **Storyboarding is commonly associated with which form of media production?**

   a. Radio journalism
   b. Print journalism
   c. Television and film production
   d. Photojournalism

6. **In profile writing, what is the primary focus of the article?**
    a. The writer's personal experiences and perspective
    b. An individual's life, character, and achievements
    c. Scientific data and research findings
    d. A fictional narrative
7. **Which of the following best describes the role of a magazine journalist?**
    a. Covering daily news events and political issues
    b. Providing quick, concise updates on current affairs
    c. Exploring diverse and in-depth topics, often through feature articles
    d. Focusing exclusively on sports reporting
8. **What is a defining characteristic of feature writing?**
    a. A strict adherence to the inverted pyramid structure
    b. In-depth exploration of topics with creative storytelling
    c. Minimal use of descriptive language and vivid imagery
    d. A focus on breaking news and current events
9. **What is a key consideration in radio journalism, given that there are no visuals to accompany the content?**
    a. The use of a traditional inverted pyramid structure
    b. The use of sound and descriptive language to engage the audience
    c. The avoidance of human-interest stories
    d. The exclusion of interview segments
10. **What is the primary goal of photojournalism?**
    a. To create visually appealing and aesthetically pleasing images
    b. To document and convey news stories and events through photographs
    c. To edit and retouch images for advertising purposes
    d. To focus solely on artistic and abstract photography

Answers

1. c. Timeliness and objectivity
2. c. Allow for creative storytelling and exploration of human interest
3. c. A longer narrative style and more in-depth content
4. c. To disseminate agricultural information to farmers
5. c. Television and film production
6. b. An individual's life, character, and achievements
7. c. Exploring diverse and in-depth topics, often through feature articles
8. b. In-depth exploration of topics with creative storytelling
9. b. The use of sound and descriptive language to engage the audience
10. b. To document and convey news stories and events through photographs

6

Media Role

6.1 Role of Media in Democracy: Introduction

The media is the fourth pillar of democracy. The media has a critical role in creating a democratic culture that transcends the political system and gradually enters the general public's consciousness. Voters rely on the political information provided by the media to make their selections. They facilitate discussion and help discover issues facing our society.

Role of media: The media can play a positive role in democracy only if there is an enabling environment that allows them to do so. They need the requisite skills for the kind of in-depth reporting that a new democracy requires. There should also be mechanisms to ensure they are held accountable to the public and that ethical and professional standards are upheld. Media independence is guaranteed if media organisations are financially viable, free from the intervention of media owners and the state, and operate in a competitive environment.

Amartya Sen sees the media as a watchdog not just against corruption but also against disaster. He said, "There has never been a famine in a functioning multiparty democracy. A free press and the practice of democracy contribute greatly to bringing out information that can have an enormous impact on policies for famine prevention. A free press and an active political opposition constitute the best early-warning system a country threatened by famine could have." Thus, it can be said that the media plays a crucial and multifaceted role in society. It serves as a vital source of information, a check on government power, a platform for public discourse, a tool for social change, and much more.

Here are some of the key roles and functions of the media

- **Informing the Public:** The primary role of the media is to inform the public. It provides news and information about events, developments, and issues on a local and global scale. This information is essential for citizens to make informed decisions about their lives, communities, and the world.
- **Watchdog of Democracy:** The media acts as a watchdog on the government, holding those in power accountable. Investigative journalism uncovers corruption, abuse of power, and other wrongdoing, which helps maintain transparency and democracy.

- **Educating and Raising Awareness:** The public is educated by the media on a variety of topics, including politics, culture, science, and health. It raises awareness about important issues and social causes, fostering informed citizens and social change.
- **Setting the Agenda:** The media plays a role in setting the public agenda. By highlighting certain issues, they can influence what topics the public and policymakers consider important.
- **Providing a Platform for Public Discourse:** The media provides a platform for different voices and perspectives, promoting open discussion and debate. This is vital for a healthy democracy and a diverse society.
- **Entertainment:** In addition to news and information, the media entertains, including movies, television shows, music, and more. Entertainment media plays a significant role in shaping cultural values and trends.
- **Cultural Preservation:** Media, especially print and broadcast media, document and preserve cultural heritage, history, and traditions. They act as a repository of cultural knowledge.
- **Mobilising and Advocacy:** The media can mobilise people for various causes, including social and political change. It empowers activists and organisations to reach a broader audience and advocate for their goals.
- **Economic Engine:** The media is a significant economic force, creating jobs, driving advertising revenue, and contributing to the overall economy. Building Public Opinion: Through opinion pieces, editorials, and commentary, the media can influence public opinion and shape perceptions on various issues.
- **Bridge Between Diverse Groups:** The media can serve as a bridge between different cultural, ethnic, and social groups by providing exposure to various perspectives and fostering understanding.
- **Providing a Voice for the Voiceless:** The media can bring attention to marginalised and underrepresented groups, helping to address issues of social justice and inequality.
- **Public Safety and Emergency Communication:** During crises, the media plays a critical role in disseminating emergency information and ensuring public safety.

- **Global Perspective**: Media connects people to global events, fostering international understanding and cooperation.
- **Technological Innovation:** Media often drives technological innovation in the communication and information sectors, leading to new platforms and ways of sharing information.
- **Fostering Public Debate:** The media provides a platform for public discourse, enabling citizens to express their views and engage in discussions about various social, political, and economic issues. This debate is essential for a thriving democracy, as it helps identify common ground and formulate informed policies.
- **Facilitating Transparency:** The media promotes government transparency by reporting on government activities and decisions. It helps ensure that government actions are open to public scrutiny, which is essential for building trust between the government and the governed.
- **Serving as a Bridge:** The media serves as a bridge between citizens and their government, facilitating the exchange of information, concerns, and grievances. It provides a mechanism for citizens to voice their opinions and hold government officials accountable.
- **Promoting Social Accountability:** Media coverage of social issues and injustices can lead to social accountability. When the media exposes problems such as human rights violations, discrimination, or environmental issues, it often leads to public outcry and pressure for change.
- **Educating the Electorate:** The media plays a vital role in educating the electorate about political processes, candidates, and issues during elections. This empowers citizens to make informed choices at the ballot box.
- **Advocating for Human Rights:** The media can serve as an advocate for human rights by raising awareness of human rights abuses, inequality, and social justice issues. This can lead to public pressure on governments and institutions to address these concerns.
- **Providing Diversity of Views:** A healthy democracy thrives on diverse perspectives and opinions. The media should strive to provide a range of viewpoints, helping to prevent information silos and echo chambers.
- **Offering a Platform for Dispute Resolution:** Media outlets can provide a platform for resolving disputes and conflicts through open discussions, debates, and public forums.

- **Supporting Civil Society**: Media outlets can foster and support civil society organizations by providing them with a platform to share their research, advocacy, and activities with a wider audience.
- **Mobilising and Encouraging Civic Engagement**: Through reporting and campaigns, the media can motivate citizens to become actively engaged in democratic processes, whether through voting, attending public meetings, or participating in grassroots initiatives.
- **Promoting Government Accountability**: Investigative journalism, in particular, is vital for revealing corruption and misconduct, leading to investigations, legal action, and positive changes in government practices. In essence, the media plays a crucial role in upholding democratic principles by ensuring government transparency, encouraging public discourse, and holding institutions accountable. A free and responsible media is essential for the functioning and well-being of democratic societies. The media holds a significant influence over society, given its ability to shape public opinion and cultural norms and inform the masses. Therefore, it carries several important responsibilities towards society:
- **Provide Accurate Information:** The foremost duty of the media is to provide accurate, unbiased, and timely news and information. This is crucial for the informed decision- making of citizens in a democratic setting.
- **Act as a Watchdog:** The media should serve as the fourth pillar of democracy (alongside the judiciary, executive, and legislature). It should keep a check on the functioning of the other pillars, highlighting corruption, abuse of power, and any injustices.
- **Promote Public Discourse:** The media should provide a platform for public debate, ensuring diverse voices and opinions are represented. This promotes understanding and aids in democratic decision-making.
- **Educate the Public:** Beyond reporting news, the media has a responsibility to educate the public on significant issues—health, environment, civic responsibilities, science, and culture.
- **Ensure Representation:** Media should ensure that diverse groups within society, including minorities and marginalized communities, are represented in content and given a voice.

- **Maintain Ethical Standards:** Media entities should adhere to a code of ethics, which includes principles like fairness, accuracy, impartiality and accountability.
- **Respect Privacy**: While there's a public interest in news, the media should also respect the privacy of individuals, striking a balance between the public's right to know and an individual's right to privacy. Uphold Democratic Values: The media should operate free from undue governmental or corporate influence.

In the modern age, the media landscape has expanded to include traditional print and broadcast outlets as well as digital, social media, and citizen journalism. These new forms of media have reshaped how information is created, shared, and consumed, bringing both opportunities and challenges. While the media plays a pivotal role in informing and shaping society, media organisations and individuals need to uphold ethical standards, maintain objectivity, and provide accurate and reliable information to fulfil these roles effectively. The role of media in democracy is fundamental and multifaceted, as it serves as a cornerstone of transparency, accountability, and informed decision-making.

6.2 Contemporary Issues Relating to Media

In the ever-evolving landscape of media and communication, several contemporary debates and issues are shaping the way we consume and engage with information. These issues have profound implications for society, democracy, and the media industry itself. Here are some of the prominent debates and issues:

- **Misinformation and Disinformation**: The rapid spread of false or misleading information, often driven by social media, has become a significant concern. Media platforms are grappling with how to combat the spread of misinformation and disinformation while respecting freedom of speech.
- **Media Trust and Credibility:** Trust in the media is a growing concern. Public perception of media outlets varies widely, and there's a need to rebuild trust in journalism and news sources.
- **Digital Privacy and Surveillance:** Concerns about data privacy and surveillance have risen with the collection and use of personal data by

tech companies and governments. The media plays a crucial role in reporting on these issues.

- **Filter Bubbles and Echo Chambers:** Online algorithms often feed users content that aligns with their existing beliefs, creating filter bubbles and echo chambers. This can lead to polarisation and misinformation.
- **Hate Speech and Online Harassment:** The digital realm has seen an increase in hate speech and online harassment, posing a challenge for media platforms in balancing free speech with safety.
- **Local Journalism Decline:** Many local news outlets have faced financial challenges, leading to a decline in local journalism. This impacts communities' access to important information.
- **Media Ownership and Concentration:** The consolidation of media ownership into a few large corporations can limit the diversity of voices and perspectives, potentially affecting the quality and independence of news reporting.
- **Social Media Regulation:** Governments and social media companies are debating the extent to which social media platforms should be regulated, especially about issues like hate speech, fake news, and foreign interference in elections.
- **Media and Democracy:** The role of media in shaping public opinion and influencing elections has raised debates about the responsibility of media organisations in maintaining democratic values and transparency.
- **Media Literacy:** With the proliferation of misinformation, the importance of media literacy education has grown. Many argue that media literacy should be part of the standard curriculum to help people critically evaluate information sources.
- **Journalistic Ethics:** Media outlets grapple with issues related to journalistic ethics, such as the balance between privacy and public interest, sourcing and verification, and avoiding bias in reporting.
- **Diversity and Inclusion**: Many discussions surround the need for diversity in media organisations to ensure accurate representation of different perspectives and experiences.
- **Impact of New Technologies**: Emerging technologies like deepfake videos and AI- generated content challenge traditional notions of truth and reality in media.

- **Media Sustainability:** As traditional revenue models decline, media organisations are exploring new ways to ensure sustainability, such as subscription-based models and nonprofit journalism.
- **Press Freedom:** The protection of press freedom is a global concern, with many countries facing challenges to the independence of the media. These contemporary debates and issues reflect the evolving nature of media in the digital age. They highlight the complexities of balancing freedom of expression with the need for accurate, ethical, and responsible journalism. Addressing these challenges is essential for the continued role of the media in informing, educating, and fostering healthy democratic societies.

6.3 Ethics in Journalism

Ethics in journalism are a set of moral principles and guidelines that govern the behaviour and decision-making of journalists and media organizations. Adhering to ethical standards is essential for maintaining the trust, credibility, and integrity of the profession.

Here are key ethical principles in journalism: truth and accuracy:

Journalists have an ethical obligation to report the truth. They should strive for accuracy and fairness in their reporting. This includes verifying facts, cross-referencing sources, and correcting errors promptly.

- **Independence:** Journalists must maintain independence from outside influences that could compromise their objectivity. They should avoid conflicts of interest, such as financial or personal interests, that could sway their reporting.
- **Fairness and Impartiality**: Journalists should provide fair and balanced coverage, giving voice to all sides of an issue and avoiding personal bias in their reporting. They should not promote their own opinions.
- **Minimise Harm:** Journalists should be mindful of the potential harm their reporting can cause to individuals, especially in sensitive situations. They should avoid publishing unnecessary private details, particularly those related to victims and minors.

- **Privacy:** Journalists should respect individuals' privacy rights. They should avoid invading private spaces or publishing private information without legitimate public interest.
- **Sensitivity to Diversity:** Journalists should be sensitive to issues of diversity, including race, gender, religion, sexual orientation, and more. They should avoid stereotypes and ensure their reporting reflects the diverse perspectives within society.
- **Accountability:** Journalists should be accountable for their work. They should acknowledge errors and make corrections transparently. Additionally, media organisations should have a clear mechanism for addressing audience complaints.
- **Transparency:** Journalists and media outlets should be transparent about their sources, methods, and potential biases. This helps audiences understand the context and motivations behind the reporting.
- **Do No Harm:** Journalists must consider the potential consequences of their reporting, especially in cases where their work could incite violence or cause harm to individuals or communities.
- **Independence from Advertisers:** Advertisers should not have undue influence over journalistic content. Journalists should resist any attempts to compromise their reporting for the sake of advertising revenue.
- **Anonymous Sources:** Journalists should use anonymous sources sparingly and only when it is essential to protect the source's safety or prevent retaliation. They should provide as much information as possible to enable the public to evaluate the source's credibility.
- **Editorial Independence:** Editors should protect the independence of journalists and not pressure them to alter their reporting to fit a particular narrative or agenda.
- **Ownership and Control:** Journalists should be aware of the ownership and control of their media organizations. The concentration of media ownership can raise concerns about editorial independence.
- **Protection of Sources:** Journalists should protect the confidentiality of their sources, even at the risk of legal consequences. This is crucial for fostering trust and ensuring whistleblowers can come forward.
- **Avoid Plagiarism:** Journalists should avoid plagiarism, always giving proper credit to the source when using others' work or ideas. Ethical considerations are essential for maintaining the credibility

and trustworthiness of journalism in an era of rapidly evolving media. Journalists and media organizations must uphold these principles to fulfil their role as watchdogs, informers, and educators within society.

6.4 Let's evaluate

1. **What is one of the primary roles of media in a democratic society?**
   a. Promoting a specific political ideology
   b. Fostering censorship and information control
   c. Providing information, facilitating debate, and holding power accountable
   d. Generating revenue through advertising
2. **In a democracy, media serves as a "watchdog." What does this term imply?**
   a. Media acts as a government-controlled entity
   b. Media constantly criticizes the government without evidence
   c. Media monitors and exposes corruption, abuses of power, and wrongdoings
   d. Media serves as a public relations tool for politicians
3. **What is one of the key responsibilities of media towards society?**
   a. Promoting sensationalism and tabloid news
   b. Exaggerating stories to increase viewership
   c. Ensuring accuracy, fairness, and balanced reporting
   d. Prioritizing financial interests over public interest
4. **Which ethical principle in journalism involves respecting the privacy and dignity of individuals, especially in sensitive situations?**
   a. Objectivity
   b. Sensationalism
   c. Privacy and sensitivity
   d. Freedom of the press
5. **"Fake news" is a term associated with which contemporary issue in media?**
   a. Media censorship
   b. Misinformation and disinformation

c. social media regulation

d. Freedom of speech

6. **Which modern challenge involves the ability of media platforms to filter and customize content based on individual preferences?**

   a. Media convergence

   b. Echo chambers and filter bubbles

   c. Citizen journalism

   d. Investigative reporting

7. **What is the primary goal of ethical journalism?**

   a. To prioritize sensationalism and clickbait headlines

   b. To manipulate public opinion

   c. To provide accurate, fair, and responsible reporting

   d. To cater to advertisers' interests

8. **Plagiarism is a serious ethical violation in journalism. What does plagiarism involve?**

   a. Citing sources accurately and transparently

   b. Replicating someone else's work or ideas without proper attribution

   c. Writing original content from scratch

   d. Using anonymous sources in investigative reporting

Answers

1. c. Providing information, facilitating debate, and holding power accountable
2. c. Media monitors and exposes corruption, abuses of power, and wrongdoings
3. c. Ensuring accuracy, fairness, and balanced reporting
4. c. Privacy and sensitivity
5. b. Misinformation and disinformation
6. b. Echo chambers and filter bubbles
7. c. To provide accurate, fair, and responsible reporting
8. b. Replicating someone else's work or ideas without proper attribution

References

A guide to organizational communication (2023). Retrieved from: Arvind (2019). Web journalism. QuoraInc. Retrieved from:

Chauhan, J. (2018). Communication and Extension Management. Kushal Publications and Distributors.

Coursera (2023). Upward communication. Retrieved from:

Development. Oxford & IBH Publishing CO. PVT. LTD.

Dhama, O.P. and Bhatnagar O.P. (2007). Education and Communication for

http://ecourseson line.iasri. res .in/mod/page/vi ew.php?i d=117649#:~:te xt=Photos%2 0 will%20often%20be%20published,which%20destroy%20 the %20 entire%20im age .

https://sen dpulse.com/supp ort/glos sary /media-mix

https://www.coursera.org/articles/upward-communication

https://www.hilarispublisher.com/open-access/the-role-of-social-media-in-journalism-87120. html#:~:text=As%20a%20result%2C%20social%20media,media%20platforms

https://www.measured.com/faq/media-mix-what-is-it-and-which-types-are-best/

https://www.quora.com/What-is-web-journalism

https://www.ringcentral.com/

https://www.skillsyouneed.com/ips/verbal-communication.html

J-Ethinomics Team (2022). Responsible journalism. J -Ethonomics. Retrieved from: https://www.j-ethinomics.org/responsible-journalism-definition/

Mathew, D (2022). The role of social media in journalism. Hilaris. Available at:

Murray, C. (2023). Balance in journalism. Become a writer today. Retrieved from: https://becomeawritertoday.com/what-is-balance-in-journalism/

Rathakrishnan, T. Thomas, M. I. Nirmala, L. (2010). Communication Techniques in Farm Extension. Scientific Publishers.

Ray, G. L. (2017). Extension communication and management. Kalyani Publishers.

Retrieved from: https://study.com/learn/lesson/organizational-communication-uses- examples. html

Rogers, K. Hartzell, S. Kwong, W (2023). Organizational communication. Study.com. Sandhu, A. S. gextyebook on Agricultural Communication: Process and Methods. Oxford & IBH Publishing CO. PVT. LTD.

Saxena A. (2011). Fisheries Extension. Daya Publishing House.

Sharma S. R. (1998). Extension Education. Osmons Publications.

Skills You Need (2022). Verbal communication. Retrieved from:

Stoltz, N (2022). Media Mix. Measured® Inc. Retrieved from

Studious Guy (2023). Business communication methods. Retrieved from: https://studiousguy.com/bus in ess- com muni catio n/# Busines s_Comm uni cation_Methods

Supe, S. V. (199 7). An introduction to Extension Education. Oxford & IBH Publishing CO. PVT. LTD.

Swan, G. (2021). Media mix. Sendpulse. Retrieved from:

University Canada West (2023). How has social media emerged as a powerful communication medium. Learningwise Education Inc. Retrieved from: https://www.ucanwest.ca/blog/media-communication/how-has-social-media-emerged- as-a-powerful-communication- medium/#:~:text=The%20import ance%20of%20social%20media,other%20parts%20 of%20the%20world.

Index